A PARAGON OF ZEN HOUSE

ASIAN THOUGHT AND CULTURE

Sandra Wawrytko
General Editor

Vol. 38

PETER LANG
New York • Washington, D.C./Baltimore • Boston • Bern
Frankfurt am Main • Berlin • Brussels • Vienna • Canterbury

Xishan

A PARAGON OF ZEN HOUSE

Translated and Commented by
O'Hyun Park

PETER LANG
New York • Washington, D.C./Baltimore • Boston • Bern
Frankfurt am Main • Berlin • Brussels • Vienna • Canterbury

Library of Congress Cataloging-in-Publication Data

Xishan.
[Sôn 'ga kwigam. English]
A paragon of Zen house / by Xishan;
translated and commented by O'Hyun Park.
p. cm. — (Asian thought and culture; vol. 38)
Includes bibliographical references.
1. Zen Buddhism Early works to 1800. I. Park, O'Hyun. II. Title. III. Series.
BQ9265.S66713 294.3'927—dc21 99-27940
ISBN 0-8204-4545-2
ISSN 0893-6870

Die Deutsche Bibliothek-CIP-Einheitsaufnahme

Xishan:
A paragon of Zen house / by Xishan; translated
and commented by O'Hyun Park.
–New York; Washington, D.C./Baltimore; Boston; Bern;
Frankfurt am Main; Berlin; Brussels; Vienna; Canterbury: Lang.
(Asian thought and culture; Vol. 38)
ISBN 0-8204-4545-2

Cover design by Lisa Dillon

DEDICATED

To
My Parents
who showed me nature's way and human way,

To
Bernard Phillips
who taught me
all that I knew,

To
My Wife, Heeshin
who is bright trust,

To
My Three Daughters;
Lynn, Linda and Caroline
who are bright, beautiful and good,

And to
My Grandchild, Brendan
who was born on April 2, 1999.

Acknowledgments

I am grateful to those administrative leaders at Appalachian State University who have supported and encouraged my professional work in Zen, particularly Drs. Harvey R. Durham, Provost and Executive Vice Chancellor for Academic Affairs, R. Clinton Parker, Senior Associate Vice Chancellor for Academic Affairs, and T. Marvin Williamsen, Director of International Programs. Their financial support for the research grant enabled me to stay in both Japan during the 1996–97 academic year and in Korea during the month of May 1999. In Korea, I observed the 2543rd birthday celebration for Gautama Buddha and visited Zen Temples where Xishan used to stay, and I meditated there finalizing this book.

Had it not been for the initiative of Dr. Marvin Williamsen to ask Dean Hajime Yamamoto, Center for International Education, Kansai Gaidai University, Osaka, Japan, to provide an academic year for me to stay in Japan and obtain firsthand experiences through encounters with Japanese Zen masters, this book would not have been revitalized. Had not both Mr. Owen Lancer, Acquistions Editor of Peter Lang Publishing, Inc., and Dr. Sandra A. Wawrytko, *Asian Thought and Cultute Series* editor, recognized the need for "a simply profound understanding of Zen with the ability to communicate it in contemporary terms," my work would not have been exposed to the reading public.

Whenever I set out to face the unknown challenges of strange lands such as China, India, and Japan, my wife, Heeshin ("bright trust") has always been together with me, always my most trusted companion and support. My students in Zen class have been helpful and stimulating. Dr. Jesse Taylor, Chairperson of the Department of Philosophy and Religion, my colleagues, and the staff members have provided basic support. To all of these, my sincerest thanks.

Acknowledgments

I am grateful to those administrative officers at Appalachian State University who have supported and encouraged my professional work in Zen, particularly Drs. Harvey R. Durham, Provost and Executive Vice Chancellor for Academic Affairs, R. Clayton Barker, Senior Associate Vice Chancellor for Academic Affairs, and T. Marvin Williamsen, Director of International Programs. Their financial support for the research grant enabled me to stay at both Japan during the 1996–97 academic year and in Korea during the month of May, 1992. In Korea, I observed the 2536th birthday celebration for Gautama Buddha and visited Zen Temples where Kishan used to stay, and I meditated there, outlining this book.

Had it not been for the initiative of Dr. Marvin Williamsen to ask Dean Kazuo Yamamoto, Center for International Education, Kansai Gaidai University, Osaka, Japan, to provide an academic year for me to stay in Japan and obtain firsthand experiences through meditating with Japanese Zen masters, this book would not have been completed. Had not both Mr. Owen Lancer, Acquisitions Editor of Peter Lang Publishing, Inc., and Dr. Sandra A. Wawrytko, Asian Thought and Culture Series Editor, recognized the need for "a timely profound understanding of Zen with the ability to communicate it in contemporary terms," my work would not have been exposed to the reading public.

Whenever I set out to take the unknown challenges of strange lands such as China, India, and Japan, my wife, Hyoshin ("Bright Heart"), has always been together with me, always my most trusted companion and support. My students in Zen class have been inspiration and stimulation. Dr. Jesse Taylor, Chairperson of the Department of Philosophy and Religion, my colleagues, and the staff members have provided basic support. To all of these, my sincerest thanks.

Table of Contents

Xishan's Preface

Long ago, students of Buddhism spoke only the words of Buddha, and they conducted themselves in exactly the same way that Buddha did. Thus, they treasured only the words of *the Sutras*. Nowadays, students of Buddhism study only the writings of secular scholars and poems of politicians. Furthermore, they copy these words on colorful papers, and decorate the papers with luxurious silks. Nevertheless, their appetite is not quenched with the voluminous writings. They merely try to treasure them with the insatiable appetite. What a difference between the ancient and the present students of Buddhism!

Although I treasure the multitudinous and holy words of all *the Sutras* whose sea is so vast and unlimited, I selected and jotted down several hundreds phrases which are most needful as the best examples of *the Sutras*. This will help and relieve the future students of a laborious task of picking up leaves through taking thick branches off the tree of *the Sutras*. Even though the selections in this book are very short and simple, their meanings are widely representative. If anyone takes this book as a guide and realizes the subtle principle of life, the living Tathagata will be seen in each and every word. Thus, it is worthwhile to take pains in reading this book. Although words without letters and strange treasure without images must not be unused, one must wait for the special frame.

Summer, the year of Jiajing Jiazi (1564)
Written by Qingzutang Baihua Daoren

Blowing Rock's Preface

In October 1965, Daisetz T. Suzuki wrote the following words as his preface to the book titled *Zen and Zen Classics* (volume four), compiled by R. H. Blyth:

> *The Zen-ke Ki-kan* by Seiko Kyujo, a great Korean master. The book was published in 1579 by his disciples. This learned author consulted some fifty books of Zen and compiled a standard text for beginners to use as a mirror by means of which they could examine themselves and discover the way to proceed in the study of Zen. For example, he advises them, at the outset, to set up before themselves a "great doubt" or question which they should strive to solve with all the spiritual energy at their command. However, he warns them to do this by appealing not to their ratiocinative (sic) resources but by waking to a hidden power (that is, "the supreme reason"), as has been referred to above. This is a significant piece of advice which ought to be urged strongly upon the beginners of Zen study.

I translated *The Zen-ke Ki-kan* into English in 1985. Since the entire book was originally written in Chinese, the title of the book was transliterated and rendered in Chinese as *The Chanjia Guijian (Essentials of Zen Buddhism* in English). Since then, I have realized the necessity to improve the old translation in the current form under the new English title, *A Paragon of Zen House*, which is literally closer to the original meaning of the title. In this new book, I deleted the original Chinese text which I made a copy of from the Beijing Library in China. Instead I used the Korean version which has less cases than the Chinese. And I added introduction with my own commentaries under the heading called "Blowing Rock's Commentary." I did not translate the cases exiting between current case LXXXIII and case LXXXIV, simply because they are so difficult for me and readers to understand. However, some of them have been explained in my various commentaries. This sixteenth century *Chanjia Guijian* has its distinct Zen spirit sung in the eighth century *Liuzu Tanjing (The Platform Sutra of the Sixth Patriarch)*, the tenth century *Chuan Deng Lu (The transmission of the Lamp)*, the eleventh century *Biyanji* or *Biyanlu* (*The Blue Cliff Record* or *hekiganroku* in Japanese), and the thirteenth century *Mumenguan* (*The Gateless Gate* or *Mumonkan* in Japanese).

In 1971, I moved to Boone, the northwestern part of North Carolina from Pennsylvania in order to teach students at Appalachian State University, which was celebrating its centennial year (1899–1999). I have resided in a little town called Blowing Rock for about thirty years. I have

have liked the name "Blowing Rock." In world literatures, nature has been frequently mentioned as the primary source of insight. For example, Wordsworth said:

> *One impulse from a vernal wood*
> *May teach you more of man,*
> *Of moral evil and of good,*
> *Than all the sages can.*

Jesus said,

> See how the lilies of the field grow. They do not labor or spin. Yet I tell you that not even Solomon in all his splendor was dressed like one of these.

Wordsworth wrote again about both stones and winds:

> *And though poor stones have neither speech nor tongue,*
> *While active winds and streams both run and speak,*
> *Yet stones are deep in admiration.*

Rocks like stones are deep in admiration. Rocks, unlike the wind, just sit still and never wobble, as if they are the presence of Tathagata. Anyhow, I have chosen "Blowing Rock" as my own nickname. I did so, not because I have embodied the spirit of the wind and nature of rocks, but because they invite me to be with them.

The wind is also mentioned in a waka which said:

> *When it blows,*
> *How noisy*
> *The mountain wind!*
> *But when it blows not*
> *Where will it have gone?*

Neither blowing nor not-blowing has any ultimate meaning in itself, until or unless one realizes the truth that both blowing and not-blowing are merely two aspects of One Thing. One Thing cannot be caused to cease, simply because it is uncreated, invisible, intangible, and ineffable.

The Bible relates the wind to the Holy Spirit:

> The wind blows wherever it pleases. You hear its sound, but cannot tell where it

comes from or where it is going. So is with everyone born of the Spirit.

A poem, composed by a Welsh poet of the sixth century A. D., also helps one to understand the nature of the wind and that of "born of the spirit."

The wind without flesh, without bone, without veins, without feet, is strong.
The wind has no wants, but the sea whitens when he comes out of nothing.
He is in the field, he is in the wood, without age, without old age.
He was not born, he has never been seen, he will not come when desire wishes.
He is loud voiced, he is mute.
He is uncourteous, he is vehement, he is bold.
He is bad, he is good.
He is yonder, he is here.
He comes from the heat of the sun, and he comes from the coolness of the moon.

Chinese names in the text are rendered in the Pinyin system adopted in the Peoples' Republic of China. The author of the book is generally known as Xishan. It means "western mountain" where he used to live. He called himself "Baihua Daoren," which literally means "a man from Baihua." Baihua is a name taken from the temple where he used to reside. After he retired from his active involvement in the Korean government, he was called "Tuiyin," which literally means "retirement." His priestly name is Xiujing, while his pen name is called Qingxu. He was born in 1520 A. D., the fifteenth year of Zhongzong, the king of Li Dynasty (1392–1910 A. D.).

At the age of nine, his mother died. At the age of ten, his father died. Having known that he was left alone, a country magistrate took him to Seoul, the capital city, for higher education. At that time, he was twelve years old. At the age of eighteen, he traveled around the southwestern part of Korea with his friends, and he decided to study the *Sutras* and Zen. He became a Buddhist monk at the age of twenty-one. Eight years later, he was passing through a little town where he heard a single cock-a-doodle-doo. At this sound, he was greatly enlightened. And he composed a Zen poem:

"One's mind does not turn grey,
Although one's hairs do."
An ancient man said.
At just one hearing of a cock-a-doodle-doo,
One's work has been done.

At the age of seventy-nine (1599), he became the leader of monk-soldiers to defend Korea against Japanese invasion. Lusong Li, a Chinese general of Ming Dynasty praised him:

The great master discarded worldly fame to cultivate Dao.
Nation being in danger, he steps out to the world.

Having recaptured Seoul, the capital city of Korea, he returned to the mountains where he used to reside. Those who followed him are more than one thousand. Disciples, who received his dharma, were seventy. When one of his chief disciples, When Siming visited him, Xishan asked, "Where did you come from?" Siming answered, "from the old way." At his answer, Xishan yelled at him, "Do not follow the old way." At this, Siming realized the truth. After Xishan delivered his last sermon to his disciples and looked at his own picture, he composed his death poem:

Eighty years ago, that resembled me,
Eighty years later, do I now resemble that?!

He died in 1604 A. D. at the age of eighty-four.

I have asked and received no help from anyone in the improving of the book; the mistakes, especially in the translations, will be ample evidence of this. But like snow on a man's coat, these errors are light, being mine own. However, my indebtedness to various books on Zen will be apparent to all trained readers. For example, I have referred often and tacitly to materials drawn from my book titled *An Invitation to Dialogue between East and West,* and Bernard Phillips's lectures delivered in our graduate classes at Temple University. Especially, I thank Bernard Phillips deeply and sincerely for his personal labor of love given to me. For this reason, I partly dedicate this book to him.

O'Hyun Park
Blowing Rock, North Carolina
January 2000

Introduction

Zen can be viewed from many angles. First, literally speaking, "Zen" means "meditation" in English. Second, objectively viewed, it is a particular sect of Buddhism. As such, it has its unique historical and geographical background with organized formalities. Third, from a deeper point of view, it is the heart and essence of Buddhism. As such, it has no doctrines or scriptures of its own, but it points to the ultimate source of all Buddhist teachings. And the essence of all Buddhist teaching is based on the enlightenment of the historical Buddha. Taken into this consideration, it is a spiritual training directed towards imitation of Buddha's own life, practice of the process of enlightenment of the Buddha, tranquilization of heart and mind, and freedom of action. All these are directed towards achieving what the historical Buddha achieved through his earthly life. Last, still more profoundly viewed, Zen transcends all particularities of Buddhism as such, and it is not one religion so much as it is religion itself in its profoundly simple intention. In other words, Zen is tantamount to the true life, authentic being or the life of integral self in which the "I" has overcome its dichotomy from itself and humans and nature. When Zen heals the dichotomies between subject and object, there is no longer anything to be called Zen. In other words, the uniqueness of Zen is "its-being-transformed-into-the-unconditional-life." And thus Zen dies out when it is realized. In other words, the unconditional life requires Zen no more than fire calls for heat. All the comments in this book have been made from the last point of view of Zen.

Zen points to all that is alive. It goes beyond books and beliefs in order to go to life itself. The intent of Zen Buddhism is to invite humankind into unconditional union with life and with oneself. Unenlightened human life exactly mirrors the outer separation from all things. In other words, the outer separation from all things is mysteriously matched by an alienation from oneself as well. Human inner life and his/her dealings with the world are both infected with unreality in the sense that one is separated from one's own self and from one's world. Both forms of estrangement, according to Zen Buddhism, are closely tied to one's ignorance of one's own true being. It is from this state of alienation from life and ignorance of self that Zen proposes to rescue the humans.

The unreal life is a life that is not fulfilled. As a gourd that is not filled to the brim with water makes noisy sounds when shaken, so if life is not filled in full with reality it does slosh. It is only when human experience of life is complete that life means everything to oneself. Human awareness of oneself as something apart from life is the symptom of one's fallen condition. Until one overcomes it, one feels oneself as a stranger. One is afraid to live in a world which one never made.

How does one come to be in this state of alienation from self and separation from all that is? Why could not the prodigal son stay at home and enjoy his father's bounty? Why had Adam to lose Paradise? Why did Infinite Perfection create this world of imperfections? Shall one say that there is no redemption without the fall? Shall one say that there is no joyous welcome without the farewell? Zen is neither prepared to linger over these questions nor over any answers. Zen is neither a question poser nor a question solver. If anyone presses Zen to respond to this, Zen would only say that one must find one's own way home, and that only then one will understand the welcome and the farewell.

To find one's way home would be to achieve a re-entry into life. The outer world would no longer be outside oneself. And nothing would be seen as simply an object, which one accepts or rejects. In the union with life, the universe becomes one's very own; one lives in it, even as it lives in oneself. It is a living whole in which the parts retain their identity as parts and yet at the same time are fully united with the whole.

Such an unconditional union with life and with oneself is far beyond anything that could be called mere reconciliation. It is simply because to be merely reconciled to one's lot, or to accept the universe, remains on the plane of dualism where there is still a separation between the human and what the human adjusts to. Acceptance as mere reconciliation is as conditioned by separation as rejection is. Neither acceptance nor rejection can be absolutely wholehearted. To-be-one-with is something beyond any kind of affirmation and denial. What it signifies is nonduality in the absolute sense of the term. The miracle of nonduality is just this that defies the laws of logic. Nonduality transcends individuality even as it cherishes and enhances individuality. In other words, Zen as nonduality overcomes separateness and yet maintains it at the same time. If the separateness is something final, there could be no real contact and no nonduality. Without separateness, on the other hand, there would be no duality for the nonduality to exist. Where nonduality exists between A and not A, it can be truly said that, although A is A and not A is not A, and at the same time, A is not A and not A is A. This is the sort of nondual union with life at which Zen aims.

Nondual union with life is perfect love. Perfect love casts out all aversion. When life is complete from moment to moment, there is no room for hatred, anger, and fear. Furthermore, there is no room for anxiety concerning the morrow. Anxiety is symptomatic of separateness from life; it is the fear that one may not attain what one hopes for or that one may lose what one momentarily clutches. The life of nonduality will continue to have pressing problems and difficulties of life. Challenge and response must always remain the warp and woof of life. However, the problems become real only when there is union with life. They are no longer projected by ego. The responses to the problems are creative and wholehearted, not forced or vacillating. That is the great difference.

So anyone who lives in union with life must sooner or later die and face death. How do Zen people die? One dies in absolute wholeheartedness. One relates to death as one relates to life; death is not something that strikes oneself down from without. Therefore, it has no terrors for oneself. One is one with one's own dying as one is one with one's own living. In some ineffable way, one is beyond birth and death even as one is born and as one dies. Eternity, for Zen, is not a posthumous state of affairs. To live in eternity is to tap the infinity of the moment.

The fallen condition of humanity is not just one's lack of information. According to Buddhism, one's ignorance and one's alienation do not stem from a merely intellectual error, which would be rectified by presenting oneself with a statement of the truth. It is one's own being that is in error. The truth of the matter is that one's own being is constituted by the error. To overcome the error one must overcome oneself. The error will be vanquished only after a confrontation with death. Every level of love entails a dying and a resurrection. The rebirth into the life of absolute love comes after what Zen calls the Great Death. No one is prepared to take that last step until one has first exhausted all his other resources, and finally stands emptied of all contrivances for meeting life. Only then will the need for reality drive oneself to the final abandoning of oneself. The practice and discipline of Zen are to bring one to this point.

The great death is also the Great Awakening. The existential awakening to one's true self is called *enlightenment*. It is the entry into the life of nonduality where one is no longer caught by the play of the opposites, where self is not set over against other. There is no final enlightenment, as there is no final perfection of love. Life itself is not final or finished. The true Zen person does not look upon enlightenment as a momentary experience after which somehow all of life's problems will vanish. What vanishes are not life's problems, but one's externalities vis-à-vis those problems. One now deals with all problems and with one's own self from within instead of from without—that is the great difference.

As one is now one with one's tasks, tasks are not to oneself mere obstacles to be disposed of so that one may begin the business of really living. One's tasks *are* one's life. One lives in the NOW, not in the abstract future. It is in the uncreative life that the doer is separated from what one does. It is one's divorce from life that makes one look before and after. One pines for what is not. Zen person gives oneself wholeheartedly to its moments. And perceives no radical difference between means and ends.

The unenlightened person always faces a choice of this or that, unable to have both and yet bound to learn sooner or later that each is incomplete without the other. One's reason opposes one's passions. One's higher nature is at war with one's lower nature. The law in the members conflicts with the law of the mind. One wishes to serve God, and yet is perennially tempted by the Devil. No ultimate peace can come to one who is thus fissured. Peace is but another name for the authenticity of being which enables one to respond to life without inner conflict. A mind in pieces cannot be a mind at peace. Every dualistic recipe for achieving the peace that passeth understanding is predestined to failure, for it entails the futile attempt of one side of oneself to coerce the opposite side into a renunciation of its own needs. Authentic self, Zen would say, is not to be sought in any dimension of oneself but only in that from which every dimension is an abstraction. Until one finds the living center of unity which is one's authentic being, one will be neither peaceful nor authentic.

The religions of the West are all dualistic. It means that they accept one half out of pairs of opposite as ultimate. Therefore, they seek for truth in halfness as contrasted with its opposite. Life itself will not for very long submit to such Procrustean treatment. The devaluated fragments reassert themselves periodically. So Western religions have never been free of the struggle with materialism, secularism, and individualism. The loyalty of the Western devotee has always been fragmented and divided.

Authenticity is wholeness, not halfness. Holiness is holistic living, not self-conquest. Spiritual freedom is unopposed response, not self-control or self-restraint. Wholeheartedness can never eventuate from the resolution to disregard or slight what is half of the reality. A mature religion must concede that both the "higher" and the "lower," both the transcendent and the immediate, are equally real, or rather equally unreal and abstract. A mature religion will courageously confront the profound mystery embodied in the dichotomy that is itself characteristic of human life, and will not seek salvation through any of the fragments resulting from the dichotomy. For Zen, the split is the consequence of standing apart from life and inspecting it objectively. The split is healed only through the reentry into life, which confronts life's totality.

Zen seeks for an absolute which is a living whole embracing all the pairs of opposites. So Zen sees religious life as the utterly concrete life which is not tangled in this insoluble dualism. The ultimate wisdom of Asia, brought to a focus in Zen Buddhism, is the perception that truth and reality must never be sought on the plane of opposition. It is the essence of idolatry to accord with what is less than the whole. Zen steers humans away from idolatry inherent in every form of partisanship. It directs a human course to the living truth which is truly all in all. The center of the circle is the focus of unity for the radii. One stands at the center and one comprehends all the radii together. It is just human off-centeredness which is a human ultimate problem.

Only one who lives from one's center of life can be called truly religious. That which characterizes the life of the enlightened soul is just that it has achieved creative wholeness. Such a life is graced with absolute freedom, for its movements are authored and authorized by the whole being. Such a one will be remarkably distinguishable from the individual whose religion is still enmeshed in either/or and whose life is conspicuously marked by tenseness and incessant struggle as one strives in vain to subdue half of oneself to the other half. The Zen life is the life of wholeness responding to life in totality.

As Xishan had already warned in his preface, it is necessary to warn the reader once more that the best book about Zen is only a book *about* Zen, but is not Zen itself. In the end, the essence of Zen must not be sought through any writings. The greatest danger of reading too much about Zen is that one may arrive at a mere understanding of Zen. When Zen is understood, it is no longer Zen that one has but only a conceptual facsimile thereof. The beginner who is not in direct contact with the living tradition of Zen must turn to the written word for at least preliminary guidance. And one can only ask that the word becomes a living word which will emerge from a deep and sustained experience with the real thing.

Case I. One Thing

There is One Thing, which has always been bright and holy; It has no beginning and no end, and It has neither name nor form.

Xishan's Commentary

What is One Thing? A man of old put it this way: "Even before the first Buddha was born, It was encircled, infinitely bright all round. Even Sakyamuni did not know its meaning. How could Mahakasyapa possibly convey It?

The old man reveals the reason why One Thing has no beginning and no end, and has neither name nor form. The sixth patriarch once asked the assembled monks, "I have One Thing which has no name or title. Does anyone know what It is?" Then master Shenhui answered promptly, "It is the origin of all the Buddhas. It is my Buddha nature." With this reply, Shenhui was now regarded as an illegitimate son of the sixth patriarch.

Having come a long way from Songshan to see the sixth patriarch, the master Huairang was asked, "What is One Thing and where does It come from?" Huairang was dumbfounded by the question. It took eight years before he found an answer. He returned to see the sixth patriarch and confronted him, saying "To call It One Thing misses the mark!" The sixth patriarch acknowledged Huairang to be his legitimate son in the light of the worthy answer he had given.

Xishan's Poem

All the saints of the three teachings
Originate from this phrase.
Who dare speak out?
Eyebrows may fall out!

Blowing Rock's Commentary

The third patriarch in the line of Chinese Zen (Chan) Buddhism, Sengchan, says in *The Shinsinming, "Perfect like great Space, It has nothing lacking, nothing in excess."* Although One Thing has different names such as the Mind, the Nature, the Truth, or the Way, It cannot be described fully. It fills the endless space. Thus, there is neither outside nor inside. It is atemporal. Thus, it has no beginning and no end. It cannot be argued that it is big, small, little, much, high, or low. It is neither false nor truth. It is neither holy nor unholy. It has no distinction. And thus, It is inevitably symbolized as a circle. Even this symbol cannot fully explain the totality of It. And thus it is said that It becomes wrong, even before one opens one's lips. Insofar as spoken words assign a finite meaning of One Thing, that is, life in totality, they cannot be ultimately adequate to life's need. As the Hindu scriptures tell, "Reality is *neti* and *neti.*" In other words, life in totality is *not this, not that*. Reality or Truth is nothing one can finally specify. One Thing that sets humans free is not to be found in any specifiable teaching.

The purpose of religion or Zen in particular is to say the last word. The last word is not any word. Every attempt to say the last word or to answer the ultimate question or to correct the mistakes of all others who have preceded us remind me of a Zen story which illustrates how impossible it is to say the last word. Four men made up their minds to go on a spiritual retreat. The purpose of their retreat was to observe silence for a week. The first day went very well. However, towards nightfall, one of the four said to a servant, "Won't you come in and light a candle?" The second said, "I thought we were not supposed to speak." The third said, "What are you two arguing about, have you two forgotten our vow?" The last said, "I am the only one who has kept the vow." The last word is One Thing before which all words shrink to nothing.

Therefore, it is said that It is beyond both knowledge and ignorance. That is the reason why Sakyamuni did not know, and patriarchs did neither receive nor transmit Its meaning. The ultimate purpose of Buddhism is not to believe in Buddha, because everybody is originally Buddha. Furthermore, one must go beyond the first Buddha. What a use to have and read the 80,000 *Sutras*, if one understands One Thing. One Thing is like *a sphere whose center is everywhere and circumference nowhere.*

Sakyamuni is one of the titles given to the founder of Buddhism. It means "silent sage of the Shakya clan." His father was a chieftain of the Shakya clan. His given name is Siddhartha (Pali, Siddharttha). Gautama (Pali, Gotama) was the family name. He was born in about 563 B. C. E. in northern India. Seven days after he was born, his mother died. His mother-in-law raised him. The young boy was possessed of a clear, analytic mind and very sensitive spirit. At sixteen, he married a cousin who was a neighboring princess. Between them, a boy, Rahula, was born.

Gautama, unlike Jesus, was endowed with everything people

ordinarily want. After having lived his life for 29 years, life finally became a serious problem to him, and he was driven to seek after its secret. The prince finally resolved to get out of the palace to find its secret. He spent the six years of spiritual quest under various ascetic teachers. He came to the realization that asceticism is not the way for him to go. He began to take care of his body. At the age of 35, he was enlightened under the Bodhi tree and became Buddha. And then he shared his enlightenment with people for the next forty-five years. And he died at the age of eighty in 483 B. C.

Mahakasyapa was a Brahmin. The literal meaning of "Mahakasyapa" means "great light." He became the first of the disciples of Buddha. He is called the first patriarch in the line of Indian Buddhism. After Buddha's death, he was responsible for editing the teachings of Buddha.

Huineng (638–713 A. D.) is the sixth patriarch in the line of Chinese Zen school. He is the third most famous personage in the history of Zen. The others are Buddha and Bodhidharma. Bodhidharma is the twenty-eighth patriarch in the line of Indian Buddhism and became the first patriarch in the line of Chinese Zen school in about 520 A. D. Huineng came from the southern part of China. His father died when he was three years old. He supported his mother by selling firewood. At the age of twenty-four, he heard a monk reciting *the Diamond Sutra*, which opened his heart. The monk encouraged him to visit the fifth patriarch Hongren who lived in Yellow Plum in Huangzhou. Huineng managed to earn money enough for the support of his mother while he was gone. When he met master Hongren, he obediently did whatever the master commanded him to do. He became rice cleaner for the monks for more than eight months.

One day the fifth patriarch made an announcement to give a Zen test. The test was to compose a poem to express the spirit of Zen. Anyone who passes the test would be given the patriarchal mantle and title as his legitimate heir. Shinshu, who died in 706, was the head of monks. He composed Zen poem and posted it on the bulletin board which says:

The body is the Bodhi tree,
The soul is like a mirror bright,
Take care to keep it always clean,
Let no dust heap up little by little.

Next morning another poem was posted alongside of Shinshu's poem. It says:

The Bodhi is not the tree,
The mirror is nowhere shining,
There is No-thing from the beginning,
Where can any dust accumulate?

This poem was composed by Huineng. To Huineng, One Thing is not any thing, but It is *No-thing*. The fifth patriarch saw in this humble monk the future leadership of Zen school and decided to proclaim him as his legitimate heir. So the patriarch invited him to come to his room to receive the robe as symbol of the Zen authority. Because of jealousy aroused in the monastery made by Shinshu, Huineng fled to the Caoci Mountain. There he taught Zen until he died at the age of 76. His teaching is known as the southern school of Zen, while Shinshu's is known as the northern school of Zen.

Shenhui (686–760) was well versed with both Confucian and Daoist writings, but he liked to read and study the Buddhist writings more than anything else. Finally he studied Zen under the leadership of the sixth patriarch who accepted him as an illegitimate heir, simply because he tried to verbally answer the question. Because of his effort to expand the southern school of Zen, the northern school of Zen was ended.

Huairang (677–744) left his home at the age of fifteen. He stayed with Huineng for eight years when he discovered his true self. He served Huineng for fifteen more years. His answer was made of his silence, which was louder than any verbal statements. In other words, what one is speaks so loudly that it is not necessary for one to speak or do. Therefore, what one is speaks so loudly that no one can hear what one says.

All the saints of the three religions refer to Laozi of Daoism, Kongzi of Confucianism, and Sakyamuni Gautama of Buddhism.

Case II. The Stirring of Ripples Without Wind

The coming of both the Buddha and the patriarch into the world is like the stirring of ripples without the wind.

Xishan's Commentary

The Buddha is Shakya Tathagata and the patriarch is Mahakasyapa. "The coming into the world" refers to the salvation of all beings through great compassion. However, in view of One Thing, every human's original face from the beginning is perfect in itself just as it is; why in the world does one want somebody else to put rouge and powder on one's face? Therefore, the Buddha's coming into the world is like the stirring of ripples. That is the reason why *the Akasagarbha (Emptiness) Sutra* said, "words are the works of mara; names and forms are the works of mara; even the sayings of Buddha are the works of mara." When one discovers one's original nature, neither a Buddha nor a patriarch can be of any use.

Xishan's Poem

Heaven and earth lose color,
The sun and the moon cease to shine.

Blowing Rock's Commentary

"All beings" refers to all living beings: The Buddha wished to save not only human beings but also all living beings as well. Mara is the evil one who hinders, kills, or destroys. Mara exists in one's mind, whenever one's own mind is in pieces.

The work of the evil one is nothing but all forms of one's attachment to things such as actions, words, and thoughts. Because of the attachment, all living being is subject to birth, old age, disease, and death. In the beginning of his pedagogy, the Buddha suggested that humans should *not* commit wrong work *but* perform good work. In the middle stage of his teaching, he taught that humans should be free from *both* wrong work *and* good work altogether. And he also taught that one should not be attached to any form of blessing or sin. Toward the end of his teaching pedagogy, he emphasized that one should not be attached to his own teaching about non-attachment. The teachings of Buddha, whatever they are, are merely outward expressions of one's original face.

People many times tend to choose and to absolutize some limited images taken out of the infinite nature of one's original face, which is perfect in itself just as it is. In this way, they pretend that a picture contains its totality. Even the sum of all its pictures of a living reality is not reality itself. The choice, the absolutization, and the pretense are always partisan and hence partial. To take any side is to possess only a side, that is, a limited truth of life itself. It is not the full living truth of life. What One Thing, that is life in itself, says to each one of us is, "Thou shall have no other gods before me." In more mundane language, "Accept no substitutes." This means that one is not to interpose words, names, and forms or the teachings of Buddha between oneself and life itself. Zen Buddhism in the deepest sense is a way of purifying oneself of all these things so that one's response may be innocent and directly related to life itself.

No doubt, all things must have names and forms. Whenever one hears the name of a thing, one can imagine its manifold forms. Regardless of its having visible form or not, its manifold forms mean not only spatial body, volume, or matter but also temporal appearing, dwelling, leaving, disappearing, becoming, or hollowing. Furthermore, they also refer to warmth, sound, color, smell, or taste. Nevertheless, forms and names have no substance. They are momentarily made by all forms of attachment which are conditioned by the law of causation.

For example, "Buddha" and "all things" are words used in a dreamy world. From the beginning, there is nothing like darkness, light, knowledge, or ignorance. And thus there is no need either to cut off any form of bondage or to be free from suffering. Therefore, there is no need to achieve great enlightenment. Originally, everybody is Buddha just as one is. One Thing mentioned in the previous Case is nothing but one's original nature or face.

Case III. Dharma

But Dharma has many meanings, and human has many temperaments. And thus many methods must be used.

Xishan's Commentary

The Dharma is One Thing; human is common people. In the Dharma there are two meanings: permanent meaning which cannot be changed, and transient meaning which is affected by the law of causation. In human being, there are two temperaments: that of sudden awakening and that of gradual cultivation. Thus, it cannot be said that there are no means of teaching with letters and words. For instance, there is a saying: "In public there is not enough space for a needle, but in private a cart can pass."

However perfectly human being may be made from the beginning; one is subject to samsara without wisdom's eye. What else could peel off one's thick shell of ignorance other than the world-transcending golden knife? Only by the compassion of the Buddha can one reach the other shore of joy across the seas of pain. So even if one was to try to repay the Buddha with one's own priceless life, it would be still less than one ten-thousandth of the debt to the Buddha. That is to say, one must thank the Buddha and the patriarchs for their boundless grace by beginning to cultivate one's own mind anew.

Xishan's Poem

As the king comes to the throne,
People sing and praise him.

Blowing Rock's Commentary

In South Asian religions, Dharma is a word with an infinite variety of meanings. In Hinduism, it is the Hindu term for their own religion which means "way of life." Considered as moral law, it means the rules for a higher life than that given for sexual or material desire. As one of the three jewels of Buddhism: Buddha, Dharma, and Sangha, Dharma refers to the teachings of the Buddha. When it is used in the plural, dharmas refer to the sense objects or events. It is also understood as the unchanging and absolute principle cherishing the cosmos. In this sense, Dharma refers to One Thing that is in all things without exception. In other words, Dharma is the normative truth. And It transcends truths in the plural as It cherishes and enhances individual truths. It is a living whole in which the parts retain their identity as part, and yet are fully rooted in the whole. In other words, Dharma overcomes separateness and yet maintains it.

Transient meanings come into being whenever any object in the world influences human senses. And thus, sensation supplies all transient meanings. According to the transient nature of the relationship between material world and self, all kinds of change and motion arise. Although the actions and reactions based upon transience vary, the essence or substance of these activities is always unchanging, calm, and unmoving regardless of places or times. And thus it is called permanence. This principle can be called Dharma, One Thing, Tathagata (thusness), encircled silence, evenness, or blown out (nirvana).

Each and every human being is different in temperaments, customs, and characters. Likewise, Buddhism can be approached gradually from many angles of human temperaments. Step by step approach to enlightenment is called gradual cultivation. To be enlightened suddenly is called sudden awakening. Although one can come to sudden awakening, it is hard to get rid of one's accumulated and accustomed lifestyles. Because of the impossibility to be free of the old habits, one has to continually cultivate oneself. Awakening has come to oneself suddenly, but it needs one's arduous and continual task. Seen from this point of view, it can be said that awakening or enlightenment, sudden or not, is never final or finished. One must further enlightenment with gradual cultivation. Siddhartha Gautama himself did not come to enlightenment without any effort on his part. At the end of deadly and futile ascetic effort, finally he came to enlightenment under the Bodhi tree. And he continued to cultivate himself after his enlightenment. In this regard, it can be said that enlightenment cannot be given from the outside or passively attained from within. It must be won.

However, without the opening of an eye which is enlightenment, one cannot rightly cultivate oneself. That is the reason why patriarchs put too much emphasis upon sudden enlightenment. According to the law of causation, nothing in the world disappears completely. Instead, everything in the world changes into different forms according to the law of cause and effect. Water is transformed into clouds. Clouds again turn into rain.

Likewise, everything in the world goes around according to the law without ceasing. All things are living through the world of their respective action or thought of love-hate and of joy-sorrow. When things in the world die, they will be reborn in another form of life. Like turning wheel, they recycle their forms of life. The present form of life is also a portion of the turning wheel of previous causation. However, the goal of Buddhism is neither to control nor to flow through the wheel of causation but to cut off the law of causation by sudden awakening.

In traditional India, medical doctors used the gold knife to conduct the eye surgery in order for helping the patients to see again. The golden knife is used as a symbol of wisdom. If one is blind, one cannot see. To the blind, the world seems dark. Likewise, to the ignorant mind, mind seems dark. Because of the ignorance, the world seems to be infinitely divided into many forms which appear to be conditioned by the law of karma. One needs the gold knife to cut off the law of causation. When one has the enlightened eye, one is released from the law of cause and effect. As *the Bible* says, *He that loses his life shall find it.* In other words, the enlightened is one who is not abashed by the law of causation.

There is an interesting story about Mohammad who made his people believe that he would call a mountain to him. The people gathered together. He called the mountain to come to him, but the mountain stood still. However, he was not abashed at all. Instead he said, "If the mountain will not come to me, I will go to the mountain." The important point here is that he was never abashed, when the mountain stood still.

Case IV. No Clinging To Names

Positively It has been called "Mind," "Buddha," or "Living Things"; but one should not make any distinction by clinging to names. All is right as it is. It goes awry as soon as one begins to think.

Xishan's Commentary

Giving One Thing three different names is unavoidable in Buddha's teaching. Making no distinction by clinging to names is unavoidable in Zen. To elevate and to suppress, or to build and to destroy, are freely given commands made by a Righteous King.

This makes an end with the former, and a beginning with the latter in order to talk about the difference between the Buddha's methods and the patriarchal devices.

Xishan's Poem

After a long drought it rains sweetly,
Far away from home one meets one's friend.

Blowing Rock's Commentary

Righteous King refers to Buddha. He expounds truth clearly. He uses truth uninterruptedly. He teaches truth without limit. Furthermore, he is the teacher of both all kings and all teachers. This is the reason why he is called the Righteous King. In other words, his teaching is not a teaching in any normal sense of the word: His teaching is not a package of ideas or doctrines in which one has to believe. His teaching is not any "—ism." In truth, there is no single teaching to be called "Buddhism."

The fundamental character of Buddhism is spiritual rather than historical. Buddhists call Buddha's teaching "Dharma." It is not seen as objective doctrine but as a way to One Thing. In other words, he teaches what he has to teach to enable one to find one's true self. He will use any names or forms to help humans find their respective true self. In the end, he eventually discards every name or form to make an end with his verbal teaching. His teaching is a pedagogical adjustment to a seeker in a particular place and at a particular moment. There are different schools of Buddhism which are suitable to different ages, different climes, and different human temperaments for helping humans to attain the enlightenment.

A much deeper understanding of diverse names such as *God, Yhwh, Allah, Sat Nam, Brahman, Atman, Buddha, Dao, or Tien* and tolerance towards different religions can be found in Zen. To Zen, diverse names and forms are real necessities for spiritual education. Truth is One Thing, but people call It by many different names. Different names are inevitable. Human approaches to One Thing are literally unlimited in number. According to Zen, tolerance towards different approaches is not just an extrinsic etiquette but an intrinsic necessity.

Case V. The Three Places

The mind of the Buddha as transmitted in the three places became Zen, and what the Buddha said during his lifetime became the teaching. Therefore, Zen is the mind of the Buddha, and the teaching is the word of the Buddha.

Xishan's Commentary

The first of the three places is the stupa where Sakyamuni shared his seat; the second is the Mount Gijihakuta where he held a flower in his hand; the third is the sal tree under which he showed his feet through his coffin. These are the places where Mahakasyapa in particular received the lamp of Zen.

The five divisions of Buddhism evolved from what the Buddha has said over the course of his forty-nine years. The first are the moral teaching to people and the gods. The second is the Hinayana teaching. The third is the Mahayana teaching. The fourth is the sudden teaching. And the fifth is the perfect round teaching. This is to say that Ananda made the sea of teaching flow. Thus, the root of both Zen and the teaching is the Buddha, and the branches of Zen and the teaching are Mahakasyapa and Ananda respectively.

To reach the place of wordlessness without a single word is Zen, and to reach the place of wordlessness with words is teaching. Furthermore, mind is the essence of Zen, while word is the essence of teaching. Though Dharma has one taste, its meanings are as different as the heaven and the earth. And thus, there are two ways: Zen and teaching.

Xishan's Poem

Don't fail to attend each step,
You will fall on the grass.

Blowing Rock's Commentary

The word, "Zen" is derived from Sanskrit word "dhyana," which means "thinking silently," "cultivating by thinking," "getting rid of evil," or "the forest of merit." And thus it usually means the work to purify the mind by the pure concentration. Seen from this point of view, Zen cannot be a sole possession of Zen Buddhism but the method of all types of spiritual cultivation. As a result of a change in a place and spiritual climate, Zen Buddhism with which we in the West happen to be very familiar gives us a very imperfect picture of the essence of Zen. In its deepest meaning it is impossible to identify Zen with any one particular sectarian teaching. Hence Zen Buddhism is not an object identifiable as *this* or *that*. However, historically speaking, Zen Buddhism as a patriarchal Zen originated with Bodhidharma, who came to China from India.

The teaching refers to Buddha's teaching, which varies according to climes, customs, hobbies, and abilities. The Buddha's five different levels of teaching have reflected his attitude towards spiritual fitness: Teachings are only various schoolings which are suitable to the different ages, climates, and temperaments for bringing human beings to the enlightenment. And thus his teaching is called "84,000 ways," which were put into words and also called *Tripitaka*.

The stupa is located at northwest of Vaisali where the Buddha preached. Sakyamuni Buddha in the middle of his preaching shared his seat with Mahakasyapa, who joined him late, although his other disciples were dissatisfied with him being late.

On another occasion, the Buddha was teaching the Dharma on the Mount Gijihakuta, where flower petals came down from the sky. He picked one petal and held it up before the congregation of monks. All the monks were dumbfounded, except Mahakasyapa, who smiled radiantly. At this moment, the Buddha said to Mahakasyapa, " I transmitted the subtle mind of nirvana and right Dharma to you."

It is recorded that Buddha's death was caused by eating poisoned food. Without complaining anything about this, he died very peacefully in the village of Kusinagara. His disciples put his body in a coffin. Mahakasyapa, who came back late from his trip afar, turned around the coffin three times and bowed his head three times. And then the feet of dead Buddha appeared to Mahakasyapa in his recognition.

If Siddhartha Gautama was enlightened at the age of thirty-five and entered into nirvana at the age of eighty, then he taught for forty-five years instead of forty-nine years.

The moral teaching of Buddha consists of the Five Precepts and the Ten Fetters. The five precepts are:

1) Do not kill any living being.
2) Do not steal.
3) Be chaste.
4) Do not lie.
5) Abstain from intoxicants.

The Ten Fetters are not to commit any evil thing with one's body, one's word, and one's thought. The Ten Fetters are:

1) Do not kill any living being.
2) Do not steal.
3) Abstain from unchastity.
4) Do not lie.
5) Avoid the double-minded talk.
6) Do not speak evil.
7) Avoid subtle and artificial talk.
8) Do not covet.
9) Do not get angry.
10) Avoid opinions.

"Hinayana" means a little vehicle which carries a few people and a small amount of luggage. Having taught the moral teaching, the Buddha taught to attain calm joy of nirvana through both the ending of thinking and emptying of the mind. These steps lead to arahatship. An arahat is a Buddhist monk who experienced enlightenment for oneself, by oneself, and of oneself. The arahat-ideal, therefore, is an egoistic cultivation.

"Mahayana" means a great vehicle, which is based on the Bodhisattva ideal. A Bodhisattva is a Buddhist sage who vows to refuse to become a Buddha, until all beings are enlightened. This Bodhisattva ideal is positive and altruistic. The essential teaching of Mahayana Buddhism is that all things, as they seem to appear, are empty and nothing, and that all distinctions are not real.

The sudden teaching says that everyone is originally Buddha, that there is neither ignorance nor enligthenment. And thus there is no need to mention the long arduous process of cultivation.

The perfect round teaching is based upon the nonduality between light and darkness, between truth and false, between high and low, between little and great, and between enlightenment and cultivation. All pairs of opposite are neither different nor the same. All things are Buddhas as they are. In other words, it is the perfect round teaching that finds within human beings a reality that is identical with Buddhahood. And it does recognize divine being substantial to the natural and the human. Furthermore, it places the final goal of humanity in attaining the nonduality between A and not A without denying either A or not A.

"Ananda" literally means "joy." He is a cousin of Gautama Buddha. He had a special talent of hearing and remembering which prevented him from enlightenment. A late tradition says that a council was called after Buddha's death, and that Ananda settled matters of doctrine. According to the tradition, Mahakasyapa was asked to recite the metaphysical views, while Ananda as Buddha's favorite disciple was asked to recite the parables and sermons of Buddha.

One day, Ananda asked Mahakasyapa, "The world-honored One transmitted to you the surplice of golden cloth; did he transmit anything else to you?" Mahakasyapa called him and said, "Ananda!" "Yes?" said Ananda. "Knock down the flagpole at the gate" said Mahakasyapa. The point is the nonduality of the calling of Ananda by Mahakasyapa and the answering by Ananda. In order to verify Ananda's enlightenment, Mahakasyapa asked Ananda to knock down the flagpole to end the spiritual duel. However, Ananda did not know the meaning of knocking down of the flagpole at the gate. Having spent three days, he finally realized the meaning. And he was allowed to attend the council meeting to complete the Buddhist Bibles.

Case VI. Losing Oneself In Words

Thus, when one loses oneself in words, both the flower holding and the smile become merely the traces of teaching. When one gains from the mind, even all sorts of the worldly gossip will become Zen, which was transmitted separately from teaching.

Xishan's Commentary

Since Dharma is a nameless thing, one cannot reach it with words. Since it is a formless thing, one cannot touch it with a mind. The very moment one tries to say anything, one loses one's original mind. If one loses one's original mind, Buddha's flower-holding and Mahakasyapa's smiles just become meaningless stories and finally become dead things. For those who gain from the mind, not only the chatters in the marketplace become good teaching of Dharma but also the songs of the birds and the cries of the beasts ring real. This is the reason why Master Baoji, upon hearing a wailing voice, danced with the delight of realization. Master Baoshou, on seeing a fist fighting, recognized the original face. The depth of Zen and the shallowness of teaching are thus made evident.

Xishan's Poem

Holding a bright jewel in hand,
Rolling it over again.

Blowing Rock's Commentary

All verbal teaching made by Buddha is contained in the Buddhist *Sutras*. Apart from his verbal teaching, Buddha also directly points at the original mind, that is, the nature of Buddha. Buddhist scriptures are the verbal expressions of the original mind. They are not the original mind. They are not of the special transmission. The essentials of Zen can be found in the following lines:

A special transmission outside the Scripture,
No dependence upon spoken words and letters,
Direct pointing to the soul of the human,
Seeing into one's nature and the attainment of Buddhahood.

These four lines may be ascribed to Bodhidharma, who brought Zen to China from India in the sixth century. Having resided and taught in China for nine years, he wanted to return to India. So he asked his four pupils to gather around him. He asked them to express their respective understandings of Zen. One of the four students said, "According to my understanding of Zen, truth is beyond dualism of yes and no." Bodhidharma replied: "You have my skin." The second said: "In my opinion, it is Ananda's seeing of the nirvana." Bodhidharma responded: "You have my flesh." The third said: "All elements are void. In my view, nothing is real." Bodhidharma answered: "You have my bones." Finally the last bowed to the master and simply remained silent. Bodhidharma commented: "You have my marrow." This last monk is called Huike or Eka, who became the second patriarch.

The truth of the story is that the whole thing is beyond logical cleverness and verbal answer. Zen is beyond verbal expression not because it is beyond words or sounds but because it is "thing-in-itself." One should not presume to be privy to the trade secrets of a thing. If so, one is violating cosmic copyright laws in revealing them to all and sundry. Life of a thing is infinite. To reduce life to a verbal system is a kind of obscenity and is indecent. Reductionism is an attempt to invade the ultimate privacy of things to parade them in nudity. It can be likened to a cosmic peeping Tom who attempts to peer into the inmost secret of the universe.

Having practiced sitting-meditation for a long period of time, master Baoji came out to the street and happened to see the funeral procession. As soon as he heard the mourners' cry, he was suddenly enlightened. While others continued to mourn, he alone playfully danced around. He is one of the disciples of Mazu.

Master Baoshou received a question from his teacher, "What is your original face before you were born?" He could not answer, but he continued to wholeheartedly reflect on the question. One day, he came out to the street and happened to see a fistfight. After the fighting, one of the fighters said, "I have lost my face." On hearing this, Baoshou was enlightened and realized the original face.

Case VII. A Phrase To Say

I have a phrase to say: Just sit listlessly without either thought or work. As spring comes, the grass becomes green of itself.

Xishan's Commentary

"Without either thought or work" is what one gains from one's own mind; it is a spiritually enlightened person who has nothing to do. What a joy! One is not tied up in knots by anything, and from the beginning one does not try to work. One just eats when one is hungry. One just sleeps when one is tired. One just strolls freely across *green* waters and *blue* mountains, and just passes easily by fishing villages and wine-selling booths. One does not mind at all whether time comes or goes. As spring comes, the grass still turns green as usual.

This reminds one to return to true mind whenever a thought occurs.

Xishan's Poem

Being afraid that there would be no one,
Oh! There is One.

Blowing Rock's Commentary

Master Nanyu originally said this case. Spring thus comes and thus goes. Likewise, the grass becomes green, not because there is a painter, but because it just happens to be green as *the river glideth at its own sweet will.*

A monk asked a master, "What is your special Zen?" The master replied: "The leaves of rootless grass on the top of a mountain are moving, though there is no wind." It is creative listlessness. It actually means the living reality that transcends both cause and effect. It comes into being when one lives from the original unity of action and oneself. In other words, it symbolizes a way of being rather than a mode of physical behavior. For example, persons like Xishan or Nanyu are able to say something that is non-dichotomous. Both the way they say it and their state of mind before, during, and after saying it are non-dual. One may be very busy with bodily activity. And yet one's mind is not moved by any cause but likened to a bright mirror or calm lake. And thus one is able to describe things as they really are without editing them. For example, Wordsworth wrote the following poem of *the Daffodils*:

They stretch'd in never ending line
Along the margin of a bay:
Ten thousand saw I at a glance
Tossing their heads in sprightly dance.

Or Baso's Poem:

The old pond.
A frog jumps in
Plop!

They see the natural things unedited. Editorial principle does not influence their vision. One should not interpret their poems. Their poems are neither mystical nor pantheistic but full of Zen. When they described them as they really are, they look at the world with their original eyes. That is sufficient, no more and no less. Seen from this point of view, Zen affairs ultimately do not depend upon the law of causation. Is there another sentence which does not belong to dualism of cause and effect? To say something which is fully descriptive or logically non-dichotomous is hardly possible. However, exclamations like "Katz!" or Zen blows or Zen poems are exceptional. The following Zen poem is non dichotomous and thus fully descriptive, no more no less: *A single cloud floating in the sky has nothing ugly about it*.

Human history cannot be always controlled by external causal manipulation. Human history can be doomed without inquiring within. Wisdom, for example, cannot be obtained from causal manipulation. Schools without any doubt can produce knowledge, but it cannot create wisdom. What a joy to realize such an intrinsic truth! The essence of Zen cannot be found extrinsically but intrinsically. One has to turn the spotlight inward. In other words, it is a way of returning to one's true self. Whenever a thought occurs, one must first return to the original mind.

Case VIII. The Gate Of Zen

The gate of teaching transmits only the law of one mind. The gate of Zen transmits only the law of seeing one's nature.

Xishan's Commentary

The mind is like a mirror in itself. One's nature is like the lucidity of the mirror. One's nature is naturally pure. One can attain one's original mind by enlightenment. Therefore, the enlightened one thought is of special importance.

Xishan's Poem

Oh! Mountains upon mountains and flowing streams!
The clean and bright look of the ancient home.

Xishan's Further Commentary

Mind is of two kinds: the original mind, and the ignorant mind that grasps only transient forms. One's nature is also of two kinds: the original nature of Dharma and the other that is in direct opposition to transient forms. Both practitioners of Zen and students of the teaching are so confused that they merely cling to names and pretend to know them. They are calling something shallow "deep," and something deep "shallow." This becomes a great disease to them, so it is essential to talk about separating one from the other.

Blowing Rock's Commentary

To see one's own nature is to realize one's true self. One deeply sinks into one's own mind and sees into one's own nature, which is not different from the nature of all external things. When one penetrates into the center of one's life, there is no inner resistance caused by broken mind. And thus one truly enjoys freedom and peace. This is to see one's own nature and attain Buddhahood. Therefore, the appropriate reason to learn Zen is neither to create a better self nor to save the ego one already has. Zen is the vision that makes a way through the world. It sees what is to be seen. In other words, Zen is to see one's true self more clearly just as it is and to see things more clearly just as they are. Shoujing, a Zen monk of the Song Dynasty (960–1279) composed the following poem which reveals the spirit of the case:

A brook streams down the mountains without any meaning,
A chunk of cloud casts its shadow down upon the villages without any thought or mind.
An iron-tree blooms,
Spring comes all over the world.

Case IX. The Root Of Mind

In *the Sutras* which Buddha taught, he first classified all the laws and then explained the principle of emptiness. In the teachings of the patriarchs, the trace ends at the thought; the principle arises at the root of mind.

Xishan's Commentary

Because Buddha is the teacher of all the ages, he taught everything in detail fully and thoroughly. However, the patriarchs mainly aimed at realization to liberate anyone on the spot. The "trace" is the trace of the patriarchs' words and the "thought" is that of a student.

Xishan's Poem

Recklessly pointing;
No arms bend out!

Blowing Rock's Commentary

Buddha had a telescopic vision to classify the nature of the universe in detail. One time he mentioned 3,000 heavens, three worlds-and-twenty-five beings. Modern science makes his view abundantly evident. Light shines at the rate of 186,000 miles per second. This is about seven-and-a-half times around the earth. Now multiply 2,000 by 50,000. This is the approximate time for a beam of light to move from one end of our galaxy to the other.

He also had a microscopic vision to describe one hundred thousandth of a piece of dust. He mentioned 84,000 minute insects in one drop of water. A recall of one well-known scientific theory today will make his microscopic vision easy to understand. Avogadro's number tells us that the number of molecules in half an ounce of water is 6.023 times 10^{23}. It is enough to make our mind bewildered. A macrocosm reflects a microcosm and *vice versa*. He also mentioned and explained 108 worldly passions and 84,000 delusions.

Finally, he taught the emptiness of all beings, including his teachings mentioned above. Therefore, the essence of Buddhism does not lie in something that can be identified with objective teachings of Buddha. Buddha's intention was to accommodate his teachings to every level of human being for the purpose of attaining the principle of emptiness. Buddha has such an elastic personality that enables his teachings to be available to all beings and to put all beings in their proper places, where they may attain spiritual liberation. Spiritual freedom comes to being only when one realizes that the best lies in emptying oneself.

The phrase "The trace ends at the thought," was originally made by master Guibong (780–841 A. D.) No one can understand the teachings of patriarchs by external means; neither explanations nor logical thoughts can convey the meaning. The trace of patriarchal sayings has to end at the student's mind. As Buddha ended his association with Hindu ascetic teachers, so patriarchs did not imitate Buddha. In other words, the real way to follow Buddha is not to imitate him but to discover one's own true self.

One of the Oscar Wilde's aphorisms makes this point more evident; *the truth ceases to be true when more than one person believes in it.* Likewise, the person of Zen does not believe in a truth which is externally formulated. One must discover and create one's own truth. In other words, one has to be one's own truth. The student's thought should not be the thought that patriarchs had thought.

Once one's mind tells oneself that *the Sutras* are Buddha's teachings, it disjoins the two. One can now think *the Sutras* without Buddha himself. This frees oneself to move the teachings of Buddha around one's conceptual world at will. In other words, the teachings of Buddha become abstracted from the concrete reality of life. And thus, they will become dead words.

As knowing how to swim cannot be separated from water, so Buddha's words should not be divorced from Buddha himself, namely, one's true self. The footprint of Buddha must be erased from one's mind in order to encounter Buddha himself. Likewise, the footprints of the Zen teachers must be erased from a seeker's mind. All the separations and all the abstractions must be removed from the mind. Only then, the true emptiness arises from the clear mind, which reflects things as they really are. Genuine peace comes into being only when one attains such a true emptiness.

Case X. The Pine Tree In Front Of Garden

Buddha spoke like a bow, while patriarchs spoke like a bowstring. The unimpeded dharma spoken by Buddha urges a return to One Taste. However, one should shake off the trace of One Taste. Only then, One Mind pointed by the patriarchs reveals itself. Thus, the saying, "The pine tree in front of the garden!" cannot be found even in the library of the great dragon.

Xishan's Commentary

"Speaking like a bow" means "being curved." "Speaking like a bowstring" means "being straight." The library of the great dragon refers to *the Tripitaka* shelved in the great dragon palace. When a certain monk asked master Zhaozhou, "What is the meaning of Bodhidharma's coming from the west?" He answered, "The pine tree in front of the garden!" This is the unique Zen.

Xishan's Poem

A fish moves, the water becomes cloudy,
A bird flies, a feather falls off.

Blowing Rock's Commentary

Although cookies are different in shape, they are of the same dough. And thus every cookie has One Taste. Siddhartha Gautama Buddha delivered about three hundred sermons to the large congregation for forty-five years. His talks delivered to small groups of people or individuals are innumerable. After Buddha died, his disciples collected his sayings according to the following clusters: monastic rules, discourses, and doctrines. They are called *the Tripitaka* (three baskets): *the Vinaya Pitaka, the Sutta Pitaka, and the Abhidharma Pitaka*. As they contain all types of truth, they are called the library of the great dragon. As they are so voluminous that their meanings are wide and deep, they are also called the sea of teaching or the sea of *the Tripitaka*.

All of his teachings like cookies are focused on a return to One Thing. Likewise, their names and forms come from One Thing and will return to One Thing. However, one must not be attached to One Taste. One must be free from One Taste, in order to realize One Mind who sees things as they really are. All teachings of Buddha are just fingers pointing to One Mind, that is, one's true self. To ring a change, they are soaps or toilet papers to release the dirt from one's true self. If they are allowed to remain, they become another kind of dirt. Therefore, one must wash off both the dirt and soaps. Otherwise, one will have the stink of Buddhism.

Zhaozhou (778–897 A. D.) learned his Zen from master Nanchuan for twenty years. When Bodhidharma came to China from India to create a new form of Buddhism, he emphasized the special transmission outside the scriptures and no dependence upon words and letters. To him, the purpose of all activities in Zen lies in seeing into one's true mind to attain Buddhahood. Seen from this point of view, an answer to the question, "What is the meaning of his coming from the west?" has to be the special transmission made by one's *own* true mind. In other words, "The pine tree in front of the garden!" is an answer created by Zhaozhou himself. His answer is unique, simply because it is beyond the traditional common sense of Buddhism based on *the Tripitaka*.

Case XI. Two Gates

Therefore, a student should first understand that in Buddha's noble teachings, there are two meanings: the meaning of the unchangeable as the essence of one's own mind and the meaning of the changeable as the appearance of one's own mind. Furthermore, one must understand that there are two gates: the way of sudden realization as the beginning of the study and the way of gradual cultivation as the end of study. Having understood all these teachings, then one should abandon them in order to practice Zen with one thought reflected on the clear mind; only then one will certainly attain something. This is the living way of ego-transcendence.

Xishan's Commentary

Except those who have deeply rooted in great wisdom, common people should not take this bold leap. The meaning of the teachings is that the unchangeable, the changeable, sudden realization, and gradual cultivation are in order of importance. In Zen, the unchangeable and the changeable, the essence and the appearance, and the image and the application are all in one thought. And they are originally contemporaneous with each other. And thus, Zen is neither what is nor what is not. It is also both what is and what is not. Therefore, the patriarchs, using Dharma apart from words, point at one thought and help others see into their own nature and attain Buddhahood. This is the meaning of abandoning the teachings.

Xishan's Poem

When it is intensely bright, a deep valley covered with cloud,
Deeply calm place, clear sky, sunrise!

Blowing Rock's Commentary

The unchangeable and the changeable, the sudden realization and the gradual cultivation, and the essence and the appearance are two names of One Thing. Unless and until this is realized, none of these is real. Having said that, it can also be said that what is unchangeable is One Thing that is needful. It is thing in itself. All the rest is changeable according to the law of causation. These are the two meanings found in Buddha's noble teachings.

To Zen, all the teachings of Buddhism are likened to a map for spiritual sojourners. Having found the way to go, they have to put the map aside and continue to travel. That is why one has to abandon the teachings in order to continue to authentically live. There is no objection to any type of teaching. Teaching is needed. One has to begin with teachings. Zen, however, asks its students to see the truth that one does not end where one begins. As Zen Buddhism says, "If you come to a town where there is no Buddha, don't remain there." If one comes to a place where there is no Buddha, that is nihilism. That is not saving power. "If you come to a town where there is a Buddha, pass on." Where there is a Buddha is the place where truth has been crystallized as the teachings of Buddha. There is no saving power either. Zen neither clings to the teachings nor rejects them. Zen enters into them.

In other words, the defect of any teachings is that all teachings are all approximate. All attempts to reduce One Thing, that is, life in totality, to a systematic teaching does not enhance or help the growth of life. It is to reduce life to poverty. Poverty-stricken religion is a kind of insanity. To deprive oneself of natural richness or living strength is to treat life with contempt.

Every teaching is same. And yet every teaching is different at the same time. There is no need for anybody to strive to be attached to either this teaching or that teaching. This is that; that is this. All one needs to do is to fully express one's own individual being through any teaching that fits one's own nature. That is the reason why all teachings are contemporaneous with each other. Contemporaneous teachings tend to lack something essential to completeness. No teaching is so important for anyone to get angry at others. In other words, they all have characteristics of being relative rather than being absolute. Therefore, one should not absolutize any one teaching chosen from contemporaneous teachings. To absolutize the relative is a kind of idolatry. To absolutize one teaching is a kind of bibliolatry.

Case XII. Living Words

A student should always search for living words, never for dead ones.

Xishan's Commentary

If one attains something from living words, one will be a teacher like Buddha and patriarchs. If one gains something from dead words, one will not even liberate one's own self. Henceforth, one should make oneself enter into realization through living words.

Xishan's Poem

Meeting Linji,
One must be an iron-built person.

Xishan's Further Commentary

Huotou has two gates: words and meanings. Searching for words refers to living words, which point to a short cut. Both the way of mind and the way of words are cut by the living words, because living words are traceless and intangible. Searching for meaning refers to dead words, which belong to the gates of both Perfect Round School and Abrupt School. They have both the way of mind and the way of word, for anyone can know and think by hearing them.

Blowing Rock's Commentary

Huotou is also known as "gong'an" or "koan." It is a quest one cannot solve externally. Huotou is no longer alive, whenever technical meanings and logical traces of words are attached to it. Dead words are to come into being whenever huotou is grasped by any technical or logical means such as brilliance, cleverness, memory, or imagination. The spirit of huotou can be felt by the following Zen story. Linji (?–867 A. D.) is one of the great figures in the early Tang history of Zen in China. He is also known as Rinzai or Lin-chi. He is the founder of the Zen School, which bears his name. He studied Zen for some years under master Huangbo (Obaku). One day the head monk asked Linji, "How long have you been here?" Linji answered, "Three years, sir." The monk asked, "Have you ever seen the master?" "No, sir." The monk said, "Why don't you?" Linji answered, "Because I do not know what question I should ask him." The head monk then told Linji, "You go and see the master and ask, "What is the principle of Buddhism?'" Rinji saw the master as he was told and asked, "What is the principle of Buddhism?" Even before he could finish the question, Huangbo gave him several blows. When the head monk saw him coming out from the master, he asked about the result of the interview. Linji sorrowfully said, "I asked him and was beaten with many blows." The monk told him not to be discouraged but to go again to see the master. Linji saw Huangbo three times, but each time the same treatment was given to him. Finally Linji thought that it is best to leave Huangbo and to see another master. And the head monk agreed. The master directed him to go to Dayu. When Linji met Dayu, Dayu asked, "Where do you come from?" "From Huangbo." "What instruction did he give you?" "I asked him three times about the ultimate principle of Buddhism and each time he gave me several blows without any reasons." "I wish you would tell me what mistake I made." Dayu said, "No one could be more thoroughly kindhearted than that dotard master, and yet you want to know where you are mistaken." At this, Linji's eye was opened to the meaning of Huangbo's apparently unkind treatment. He exclaimed, "After all there is not much in Huangbo's Buddhism!" Dayu at once seized Linji's collar and said: "A while ago you said you could not understand and now you declare that there is not much in his Buddhism. What do you mean by that?" Linji, without saying a word, punched Dayu's ribs three times with his fist. Dayu loosened his hold on Linji and remarked, "Your teacher is Huangbo; I am not all concerned with the whole business." Linji returned to Huangbo, who asked him, "How is it that you are back so soon?" Linji responded, "Because your kindness is much too grandmotherly." Huangbo said, "When I see that fellow, Dayu, I will give him twenty blows." "Don't wait to see him," said Linji, "have it now!" So saying, he gave the old master a good slap. The old master laughed heartily. See case LXXIX for further development of the Linji School.

Case XIII. Cracking A Gong'an

When one studies one's gong'an, one must study it wholeheartedly. Just as a hen is hatching her eggs, just as a cat is catching a mouse, just as a hungry person is thinking of food, just as a thirsty person is thinking of water, or just as a baby is yearning for mother. Eventually, a day will come to crack the gong'an.

Xishan's Commentary

Patriarchs' gong'ans are about seventeen hundred, such as the following: "A Dog has no Buddha nature"; "A pine tree in front of the garden"; "Three pounds of hemp," and "Dry dung stick." When a hen is hatching her eggs, she keeps her eggs warm; when a cat is catching a mouse, its mind and eyes do not move. Whenever persons who are hungry, thirsty, or needy, are thinking of food, water, or mother, all their thoughts are from the bottom of their hearts. It is because their minds are not against their own will and feeling. Without this kind of sincere mind in Zen, there can be no realization.

Blowing Rock's Commentary

To the question, "What is Buddha?" Dongshan of Yunmen school of Zen answered, "Three pounds of hemp." To the same question, Yunmen answered, "Dry dung stick." These two answers are profoundly simple or simply profound. The supremely important thing in life to Zen masters is whatever they happened to be doing. A pupil approaches a religious teacher and asks: "What is the highest teaching of religion?" To this question, the teacher replies with another question: "have you eaten you breakfast yet?" "Yes." "Then go and wash your bowls." And that is all there is to religion: nothing special, no special place, no special ritual, no special prayer; just go and wash your bowls. However, one must *wash* them and not merely wash them. In other words, the means and the end are one. When one asks the question, "What is Buddha?", one must realize that the question has to be real. Otherwise, there is no answer. When one asks that question with one's own guts, then the question will answer itself. When one cannot live anymore unless one can answer that question, then the question is real. The real question is the answer. But if one just chirps the question, one is not really asking the question. It is simply because the question is not sincere. When the question becomes real, sincere, and true, one's whole being gets thrown into the question, then one will find the answer in the asking of the question. On the other hand, if one asks the question insincerely or half-heartedly, it cannot achieve the effect that one seeks.

Case XIV. Three Essential Things

There are three essential things in the practice of Zen. The first is great faith. The second is great will. And the third is great doubt. If any one of these is missing, Zen becomes useless like a cauldron with one broken leg.

Xishan's Commentary

Buddha said, "Faith is the root of attaining Buddhahood." Master Yongjia (665–713 A. D.) said, "Above all things, a student of Dao must have a strong will." Master Mengshan said, "It is a serious problem that a Zen student does not doubt gong'an." And he added, "Great enlightenment comes from great doubt."

Blowing Rock's Commentary

Faith, as usually understood, is the suppression of doubt. Zen is not a matter of faith, because faith is a partial response. And thus it cannot be a basis for any kind of absolute salvation. The reason one has to have faith is simply because one doubts. In other words, if one did not have doubt, one would not have any faith. In this sense, the faith is the covering up of the doubt or the pushing of the doubt to the rear of one's mind. As a result, there is the struggle between doubt and faith. Seen from this point of view, there is no such thing as a wholehearted belief in God. Only *irreligious* people *believe in* God. A religious person is *united* to God. Faith or belief is taking a stand on some one or idea that one has worshiped or formed. When a believer says Buddha or God, one can never be able to say the name with one's whole heart or one's whole being. If you listen to one's voice as one tries to pronounce the name of God or Buddha, you will hear that only part of oneself is saying "God," and another part of oneself is saying, "I don't believe it." That is little faith.

Great faith or right faith is spiritual. It, unlike little faith, is a trusting of the spirit by withdrawing from reliance on systems, techniques, clues, keys, images, or scriptures. The trusting of the spirit is not merely the root of attaining Buddhahood but also Buddhahood itself. The irreligious person, that is, a person of little faith is untrusting. That is, one trusts only one's own cleverness, one's own tangible accumulations of knowledge and keys. In order to overcome the problem of little faith, one must doubt about the nature of one's little faith. This is great doubt because it becomes directed toward one's own self. At the final stage of great doubt, one does not *have* any doubt but *becomes* the doubt. As Mengshan, a monk of Yuan Dynasty (1279–1368 A. D.), said, "Great enlightenment comes from great doubt."

The main purpose of Zen training is not to let students be debarred from coming to grips with life in a spiritual way. Zen is life itself, which is infinitely *beyond* human power to manipulate. Therefore, genuine religiosity comes into being only when one realizes that there is no clue that will give oneself power to control over life. True religiosity will inevitably generate "fear of the Lord," which is beginning of wisdom. Zen comes not as a very happy occasion but as a very disquieting realization that one has only a few years at one's disposal to learn one's way around or to achieve some kind of adequacy in relation to it. A person of Zen is anyone who is able to *endure* this disquieting thought. In other words, this takes courage, that is, the courage to be. This is great will. And thus a student of Dao must have a strong determination to concentrate on one's life-problem wholeheartedly. The root of all the problems in life is the gong'an, *"Who or what am I?"*

Case XV. Without Ceasing

Every day, and even in the middle of one's work, one must think exclusively over the gong'an without ceasing, "Why does a dog have no Buddha nature?" And then the way of reasoning ends and the way of meaning disappears. It is the time when everything becomes tasteless and one's mind is agonizing. That is the very place where one should give up one's body and life. That is also the foundation for one to become a Buddha or a patriarch.

Xishan's Commentary

A monk asked Master Zhaozhou, "Does a dog also have a Buddha nature or not?" He answered, "No." This one word is a gateway to Buddhahood, a tool with which one destroys all the bad knowledge and false acquaintances; it is the face of all Buddhas and the bone marrow of all patriarchs. Only passing through this gateway, can one become a Buddha or a patriarch. An old man recited, "The edge of Zhaozhou's terrible sword flashes like white frost. Whatever you ask, your body would be severed in two."

Blowing Rock's Commentary

How can any one ponder exclusively a gong'an without ceasing? How is that possible? If one spent the whole day thinking of one thing, would not it be destructive of life? If one thinks of gong'an as one special activity of life, to think unceasingly would crowd out all the other necessary activities. To think a gong'an without ceasing means that one seeks the truthful essence of whatever one has to be doing. One does not merely perform one's tasks at hand. One does not circumvent one's gong'an and problems for objective solutions. One seeks for a real relationship with whatever needs to be done. One seeks to follow the leading of the spirit in the very situation, until one lets the gong'an be the way. To think of gong'an unceasingly means in the words of Ecclesiastes, *Whatever your hand finds to do, do it with all your might*. Seen from this point of view, seeking is the whole thing, no more or no less. It is not just half the fun but all the fun.

One of the greatest weaknesses of the religious understanding of many western people is that they overestimate the answer and do not take questions very seriously. Religions today have ready-made answers to the questions, which many people have forgotten how to ask. In Zen, an answer is no longer an answer, unless one has first asked the question. A real answer comes out of a real question. The two cannot be separated. The more real the question is, the more real the answer is. The real seeking is the finding. There is no finding apart from the seeking. The seeking, unlike a hide and seek game, is real seeking, not just seeking with the intellect such as reading books on Zen.

Case XVI. An Old Mouse Entering The Horn Of A Rhino

One should neither try to understand the gong'an nor try to figure it out. Furthermore one should not wait for enlightenment. Instead, one continues to think until one can think no more. And then one's mind will be trapped like an old mouse entering the horn of a rhinoceros. It is the delusion to think that the gong'an is this or that. It is the deception to let one's life flow according to the law of karma. It is also ignorance to fear and to be confused. Ignoring the root of their troubles, the present day people are floundering in this sea of delusion.

Xishan's Commentary

There are ten diseases in studying gong'an:

1) To try to know by discrimination.
2) To be attached to the behavior that the eyebrows move up and down with the blinking eyes.
3) To earn a livelihood by sophistry.
4) To prove something with quoted words.
5) To try to figure the gong'an out.
6) To sit in a workless place after giving up everything.
7) To know by dualism of being and non-being.
8) To know that nothing really exists.
9) To pretend to know that Dao is just so.
10) To await realization impatiently.

Separate oneself from all these ten diseases. When one is meditating the gong'an wholeheartedly, one should simply doubt: "What is its meaning?"

Blowing Rock's Commentary

Gong'an is a very remarkable pedagogy to help students of Dao enter into life itself. It intends to purify people from all nonessential stuffs that exist between students themselves and life. Especially, all gong'ans are intended to rid the students of all devices. Gong'an in essence is a problem which one cannot solve, insofar as one remains *external* to it. So long as one approaches it intellectually. No kind of brilliance, no amount of cleverness, no amount of ritual activities, no amount of brilliant memory, no kind of moral activities, and no amount of imagination can figure out, recall, or imagine an answer to a gong'an. It is a problem which rejects every technical approach. In this way, the gong'an brings the student to the end of all one's ordinary objective resources. Usually, one is accustomed to dealing with problems which do not demand of giving oneself fully to them. Whenever one uses one's cleverness, one's intellect, or one's memory, one is using only a part of oneself. It is just this habit of using only a part of oneself that gong'an wants to break.

Gong'an wants one to learn what it means to lose oneself completely or to give oneself in truth. That is the reason why Zen teachers or any genuine spiritual teachers give the student a task which cannot be solved, insofar as one withholds any part of oneself from the task, that is, the gong'an. As long as one remains external to the gong'an, one will never encounter its reality. Every answer which student brings to the teacher will be sternly rejected as just another gimmick. As student continues to work at the gong'an, one becomes more and more pure in the sense of becoming progressively more free from gimmicks, more and more helpless, more and more at a loss. It is only when one is devoid of all resources that one becomes poor in spirit and pure in heart. When one is utterly purified in spirit, only then the kingdom of heaven is one's *own*.

Case XVII. To Bite An Iron Bull

This matter is likened to a mosquito which tries to bite an iron bull. One risks one's life to bite the impenetrable hide. All of a sudden, whole body will get through.

Xishan's Commentary

This is to encourage those who learn living words not to step backward. An old man said, "Zen meditation is to penetrate the barriers of patriarchs; profound enlightenment is to cut off the way of mind."

Blowing Rock's Commentary

To do anything at all at the risk of one's life does not have any reference to the strength of one's muscles or to the stubbornness of one's will but rather to the wholeness of one's heart. To live with one's gong'an, for example, is to do it without inner resistance. It is to do with undivided being. This kind of might is not the result of a try. If one does not succeed, try again. Never make any mistake about this matter. One does not decide to be wholehearted. In other words, one does not make up one's mind to be nice to others. Every such decision is only the determination of a part of oneself, which opposes a contrary impulse within oneself. There is no possibility of engendering wholehearted might by any kind of psychological stratagem. Zen enlightenment commences only when one ceases to look for such. As far as intellectual understanding goes, Zen realization is an impossibility. The undivided person, that is, the holy person, achieves this impossibility.

No one ever achieved the stature of the enlightened by conformity to teachings of patriarchs. No one ever achieved the stature of a holy person by intellectual stratagem. A person of Zen is able to penetrate one's own problem in such an intimate way as to reach its inmost spirit. One does not get closer to Zen by conforming oneself to any external teachers. Furthermore, one cannot attain enlightenment by one's own mind. One does not get to reality by moving backward or forward or sideways. The truth of the matter, according to Zen, is to get *into* it. In relation to whatever Zen school is, one finally finds to be most congenial to one's nature. The task of Zen students is not to stay with it but to get into that teaching. One may try on the garments of different creeds to see which best fits oneself. To be sure, some will fit one better than others. However, one will find that it is still an external. That is to say, one has to take it off at night. It is not really one's own or rather not really oneself. Seen from this point of view, one will never make any headway with the real tasks, which are both to penetrate through the teachings of patriarchs and to cut off intellectual understanding. The purpose of religion is not to try to prove to the world that one's religious teaching is intrinsically superior to others.

To cut off the way of mind can be likened to the Great Death. When one gives up to be just the little ego, one becomes one with one's true self, which is spiritual. In seeking to open to the self which is beyond all images that mind can imagine, one becomes more and more free of the restraints imposed by one's own mind. One becomes more open to one's true being.

Case XVIII. Adjusting The Strings Of A Harp

The study is likened to adjusting the strings of a harp. They have to be just right: neither too tight nor too loose. When one tries too hard, one is excessively obsessed with it. On the other hand, if one is forgetful, one lapses back into ignorance. Study attentively, clearly, and without ceasing.

Xishan's Commentary

Harp players say that one can get clear notes only when the strings are neither too tight nor too loose. It is the same with the study. If one hastens, the blood will become excited; if one forgets, one will stall and fall into a ghost's cave. Profundities lie where the study is neither too slow nor too fast.

Blowing Rock's Commentary

One of the Buddha's disciples tried very hard to get enlightened, but he failed and was very disappointed by his failure. One day, Buddha called him and asked, "Had you ever played harp before?" He said, "Yes." And Buddha asked, "How was the sound when the strings were too tight?" He answered, "The sound was cut off." Buddha asked further "What then if they are too loose?" He answered, "There is no sound either: The clear sound comes only when the strings are just right." Buddha responded to him, "It is the same with the study: If you study too hastily, you will be sick out of being restlessness: If you are too slow in study, you will become lazy: Therefore, study steadily." Having accepted Buddha's advice, the disciple continued to devote himself to the study and finally was enlightened.

This story affirms the spirit of the middle way. The deepest meaning of the middle way is to be found in the unity of opposites. Enlightenment is discernible neither in making haste nor in sluggishness nor through compromise between them, but only in integral life, which is not thus sundered. *What has been from the beginning joined together, let no man rend asunder.* It is the living synthesis of activity and passivity. This living synthesis is nothing but creativity. Creativity stems neither from the side of the agent alone nor from the side of passivity, but from a fructifying union between them. In this creative union, the bifurcation of human action and human passivity is existentially overcome. And the offspring of such a union will bear the mark of enlightenment.

One of the many touchstones of the union of passivity and activity is the manner in which one relates oneself to life itself. Only when one is totally reconciled with life, one does neither reject nor accept life. Instead one just lives life completely. When one is young, one puts up a lot of activity to revolt against life. One thinks that one can change life overnight. However, when one gets a little bit older, life begins to become too much for oneself. And thus one becomes mellow and passive. A certain amount of passivity or resignation is supposed to be a symptom of maturity. If a person shows too much exuberance about activity after one passes middle age, people wonder when one is going to grow up. So activity such as resistance or revolt is supposed to characterize the naive optimism of the young, while the mellow passivity is supposed to be characteristic of maturity.

Nevertheless, neither activity nor passivity is the same thing as love of life, simply because one without the other becomes either too tight or too loose. Instead, a person, who loves life, does what can be done when it can be done, and one lets the rest go and accepts the whole thing just as it is. Union with life is active passivity or passive activity. Therefore, life itself is not a problem to the person who is enlightened. There may be plenty of specific problems in life, but life itself is not problematic to an enlightened person.

Case XIX. The Army Of 84,000 Maras

When the study reaches the point where one does not know whether one is walking or sitting, then the army of eighty-four thousand maras stationed at the doors of the six senses arises as one's mind pleases. However, if the mind is unmoved, what harm can this battle do?

Xishan's Commentary

"The army of maras" is the name for the demons taking pleasure in the cycle of life and death. Eighty-four thousand maras are eighty-four thousand worldly passions. In the beginning, there was no seed of maras. But as a Zen student loses the right thought, the maras appear to be born. This does not matter for ordinary beings, because they surrender to their environments. The maras, on the contrary, attack the students of Dao, because they revolt against their environment. So they say, "As Dao is heightened, the power of maras is increased." During meditation, chopping of one's own legs upon seeing a mourner or holding of one's own nose upon seeing a pig is due to one's deluded mind, which caused oneself to see maras externally. However, if one's mind is not moved, all of maras' talents will be as futile as an attempt to slice up water or to blow out the sunlight. An old saying goes, "The wind comes through a crack in the wall, and maras creep through a crack in the mind."

Blowing Rock's Commentary

"Eighty-four thousand" is a common phrase found in the Buddhist scriptures. According to Buddhist teachings, one's deluded mind can be divided into eighty-four thousand branches. And thus there are eighty-four thousand maras as the result of representing each branch of the deluded mind. There are also eighty-four thousand ways to control them all. In India, whenever they want to express a large quantity of anything, they used to use the phrase "eighty-four thousand" or "eighty thousand." The expression "eighty thousand *Pitakas*" has derived from this source. Six senses mentioned in the case are eyes, ears, nose, tongue, body, and mind.

"The right thought" is any thought which is not dwelling on anything whatever. It comes into being when one thinks only, entirely and completely of what one is doing at the moment. Otherwise, maras will creep through the wrong thought, which is "a crack in the mind."

A monk, a long time ago, sat and meditated. Having been totally immersed in meditation, he was deluded to carry a corpse in his arms. In his delusion, a mourner came to him saying, "Why did you kill my mother?" In the middle of quarreling with him, the monk chopped the mourner with an axe. In actual fact, he was chopping his own legs from which he was bleeding. Another monk was in the middle of his study. Having immersed in his study, he was deluded to see a hog chasing him. And he held the hog's nose and yelled at the hog. After he awoke to his full mind, he found out that he was holding his own nose. This proves that maras come into being, whenever one's own mind is on the very verge of enlightenment. In other words, as Dao is heightened, the power of maras is increased. However, maras are nothing but the figments of human mind. There is nothing to worry about.

Case XX. Worldly Passion Maras

Moving minds are the heavenly maras, while unmoving minds are the earthly maras. Both moving and unmoving minds are worldly passion-maras. However, all these things originally do not exist in our right dharma.

Xishan's Commentary

In general, no-mind is the way of Buddha. Making distinction is the work of maras. The work of maras is the work of a dream. There is no need to talk about it any further.

Blowing Rock's Commentary

Zen properly conceived and properly pursued is not the pursuit of choosing something out of differentiated fragments of one's life. It is the attempt to come into total adjustment with life. A truly enlightened person is not the thinker of life but the lover of life. Whenever one's mind starts to think of attaining enlightenment, the heavenly devil comes into being. On the other hand, to love means to be in creative union with. Nothing exists in creative union with life. Where love is wanting, there are all sorts of thought, such as hatred, lust, grasping, greed, anger, fear, ignorance, distance, separation, standing outside, not getting involved, or not getting engaged. Seen from this point of view, the student of Zen is a lover of life.

Whenever one's action is from one's wholeness, it is loving or holy. To the extent that there is love in any human activity, one has wholeness responding to wholeness. So an irreligious person is a partial person or a fragmented person. One stands outside of oneself. One is not fully together with oneself. One lives and acts and responds always from some fragment of oneself. Whatever one does, one's response is only partial. Therefore, one's response is not true. One is of the devil's party not because one is guided by some kind of a gassy or shadowy figure but because there is a split in oneself between the heavenly and the earthly, a crack between passions and mind, and a schizoid tension between the moving and the unmoving. *The way is not difficult, but do not make any distinction.*

Case XXI. Karma

If one passes the most serious moment in the study without being enlightened during this life, one will not be drawn to any bad karma during the last moment of this life.

Xishan's Commentary

Karma is dark ignorance,
Zen is bright wisdom.
Is it not a matter of course that something dark
Does not coexist with something bright?

Blowing Rock's Commentary

Ordinarily speaking, karma is either good or bad. Good karma is better than bad karma. Whether it is good or bad, it is dark ignorance. Therefore, Zen is not to choose good karma as over against bad karma. Whenever goodness is viewed as opposed to badness, it becomes a basic form of ignorance. Zen does not stand on any side. Real goodness is not just the suppression of badness. If one's goodness is merely the suppression of one's badness, then it is half-hearted. Any action that is half-hearted is dark ignorance. In other words, half-heartedness comes into being, when something coexists with its opposite in oneself.

Bright wisdom is not just conformity to a good karma or a law laid down by Buddha or patriarchs. Conformity means there is some forcing in oneself. Part of oneself is trying to make the other side of oneself conform. Though the forcing may not be evident on the surface, it would come out in a psychiatric examination. Furthermore, it would be evident to the eye of any trained student of human nature. Because of its coexistence with its opposite, one's behavior will lack real ease. Real ease comes only when one's action is wholesome. If one thinks of Zen as belonging exclusively to something partial rather than one's whole self, then one's own self is divided and one is plunged into a conflict between badness and goodness. Zen dissolves the split between them. Zen embraces them both in a living harmony where there is no need to coexist. As Jesus said, *Unless your righteousness exceeds that of the Scribes and Pharisees, you will never enter the Kingdom of Heaven.* One has to break out of relative goodness by way of tasting the unique flavor of badness.

Case XXII. Questions

A Zen student should always reflect on the following: Has one known both the depth and height of the fourfold grace? Has one known the fact that this defiled body, consisting of the four great elements, is decaying without ceasing? Has one known that one's life depends upon a single act of breathing? Has one ignored and bypassed a Buddha or a patriarch, even though one met them? Has one ever forgotten for a single moment the thought that it was joyful to hear the high and holy dharma? Has one as a Zen student ever remained faithful without leaving the Zen training place? Has not one killed time by chattering to neighbors idly? Has one busily been making quarrels? Has one always been aware of the gong'an clearly? Has the gong'an continually been working even in the middle of talking with another? Has one become the Great Doubt Block even in the middle of seeing, hearing, and knowing? Can one catch up the Buddha and patriarchs when one reflects on the study? Can one definitely link up with the wisdom of the Buddha during this life? Has one reminded oneself of the sufferings of the hells when one feels comfortable in sitting and lying? Can one's body get out of this cycle of life and death? Does not one's mind wobble even when the eight winds blow on oneself?

All these things are ways which Zen students should check from time to time. An old man said, "When or where will I be liberated, if I am not liberated in this lifetime?"

Xishan's Commentary

"The Fourfold Grace" is that of one's parents, one's king, one's teacher, and one's donor. "The four great elements" are as follows: the watery element that consists of the drop of both the father's semen and mother's blood; the solid element that consists of bone and flesh; the fire element that does neither decay nor melt, after both semen and blood have come together in one; and the moving element that breathes in and out through one's nostrils.

Ananda said, "Things that are filthy and rancid are clustered together by the wild and impure passions." And thus the body is defiled. "Constantly decaying" means that time does not stop even for a moment. And thus the face becomes wrinkled, and the hair becomes silver. As an old saying goes, "I am no longer as I was. Yet I will not be as I have been." How ephemeral this body is! How horrifying it is for the fleeting demons to take pleasure in killing!

Breathing-out is the fire element, and breathing-in is the wind element. One's life depends merely upon this breathing-in-and-out. "The eight winds" are divided into two environments: one in accordance with mind and the other in opposition to mind. As for "the sufferings of the hells," sixty kalpas of human lifetimes become one day in hell. And thus, it is virtually impossible to describe the sufferings led by the boiling iron, flaming coals, mountains of swords, and forests of spears. The chance to be born as a human being again is as difficult as finding a needle fallen in the sea. That is the reason why I warn people.

Xishan's Further Commentary

As only those who drink water know if it is hot or cold, so the dharma mentioned above reveals both the fact that the intellect cannot prevent karma from arising and that dry wisdom can never free oneself from the painful samsara. Everyone should do one's own reflection and meditation, and not delude oneself.

Blowing Rock's Commentary

What is required of a Zen student is a response of whole being to wholeness. Nothing which stems from a partial dimension of oneself can generate enlightenment. For example, no question that comes merely from the intellect or calculation will be true or real. No question that comes from feeling is real. So Zen question is neither an intellectual matter nor an affair of emotion. Zen as the quest for enlightenment can never merely be the cultivation of any part of human being. Zen is neither just dry wisdom uprooted from one's own life nor just a matter of information of having a certain set of ideas about life. Furthermore a Zen quest is not just a matter of a wet emotion, just a funny, inner psychological feeling, for feeling is something that comes and goes and is not at one's beck and call. As feelings cannot be counted on and cannot provide an absolute basis for life, so all ideas also cannot be an absolute basis for life. Neither in dry wisdom nor in funny feeling does Zen have its basis.

Things begin to look black. One has exhausted all conceivable methods to find Zen solutions. One has nothing left. One is about to fall into a bottomless pit with nothing to hold on to. One begins to tremble.

In Zen, this is called the Great Doubt Block.

One's meditation and one's reflection must be made to bring oneself to this final point of a cul-de-sac. A true reflection on those questions or gong'ans must be forged in the context of one's own quest. Furthermore, one's own questions rooted in *one's own life* must have a hand in forging an answer: *Let the dilemma be the way*. In other words, life must pull the strings and call the tunes. The truth of one's own life must not be the truth about life but the truth of life. In Zen, it is said that "borrowed plumage does not grow." If one must want to soar, one must sprout one's own wings.

Case XXIII. Learners Of Words

Whenever learners of words talk, they seem to be enlightened. However, whenever they face the reality of life, they become stupefied. To them, there is an inconsistency between word and action.

Xishan's Commentary

This phrase is related to the previously mentioned remark about the meaning of deluding oneself. Talking is of no use, if it is not in accord with action.

Blowing Rock's Commentary

The majority of people do not really try very hard to make their life in accordance with their own words. They may explain to the other that these are the meanings of their own words. The explanations of their religious statements may differ to some extent, but the people themselves do not differ very much. If there is any difference, it is that between tweedle dum and tweedle dee. The persons, who say that these are the teachings of their religions, have not really made them *their own*. They have not made themselves over in accordance with the teachings. For the majority of people, there is either an unawareness of developing an unqualified allegiance to their sermons. Or there is a kind of hypocritical pretense that it has been done. In neither case, one gets really living consistency.

Zen defines religion as the living consistency between word and action. Religion has to be united with daily activity. Religion is not a dry theology but the union with everyday compassionate activity. Theology is valuable, only insofar as it exists for compassionate action. Hypocritical pretense is rooted in the separation of word from action. Whenever one realizes the living consistence, it must include both wisdom and compassion. Whenever it is not present, one becomes either ignorant or hypocritical. The nonduality of word and action is the road to heaven. The inconsistency between word and action is the road to hell.

Zen intends to bring to this point where one has got to have both not as two but in living unity. Zen means finding that very living center where one is not pulled by these two halves going in opposite directions.

Case XXIV. Cracking One Thought

If one wants to fight against the cycle of life and death, one should crack this one thought. And then one can be totally liberated from the cycle of life and death.

Xishan's Commentary

Snap is the sound of cracking a lacquered chest. Only after cracking the lacquered chest, one will end the cycle of the rebirth. It is the only way all the Buddhas began to practice.

Blowing Rock's Commentary

This one thought is likened to a lacquered chest, which is nothing but one's unenlightened ego. The unenlightened ego sees the world, but does not recognize the truth; just as a bug does not know that it is in the pitchy dark lacquered chest and goes round and round. Furthermore, it is amalgamated with three poisons; desire, aversion, and ignorance. One has locked it so tightly that no one can unlock it except one's own snapping out of itself. There is no external key to release it. Without cracking one thought, one does not feel very good. And anxiety hovers around its edge. In other words, one feels darkened and suffocated. And thus one feels stuffy and becomes unstrung. To others, this one thought is trivial, ego-centered, dull, weary, and secretive.

It is breakable, because it is subject to change and suffering. In other words, this tight and compressed chest is inevitably for the fall. However, if one accepts the snap gracefully, there must be an opening made by the sound of breaking without coming to pieces. This opening is the dawning of spiritual liberation.

Again, this one thought can be likened to shadows found in Plato's allegory of the cave. The shadows that the prisoners see are certainly real in that they exist in some sense and to some degree. However, the objects that project the shadows are more real. In this sense, objects embody more life, simply because objects possess three dimensions rather than two dimensions. When one of the prisoners manages to escape from the cave, the character of shadows is nothing but the relative absence of light. To the free prisoner, the light can be directly seen. This is the time when the enlightenment dawns.

To produce a change on Plato's allegory of the cave, the one thought can be compared to a stained glass-window. The stained glass window reflects what lies outside opaquely. Those who stay within may have a dim view of the outside world. They may have to believe in what they are told by others who are outside of the building. Therefore, they realize that everything within is neither more nor less than a reflection of what lies outside. So they may develop a tendency to direct their sense of orientation toward a transcendental world. Furthermore, there are some who, without changing their sense of direction, merely *open* the opaque stained glass window, and are able to see things as they really are. They do not need to go anywhere. This last level is where one cracks the one thought and where the very enlightenment dawns; a crack of spiritual dawn.

Case XXV. Seeking For An Enlightened Teacher

Even after one has cracked one thought, one should seek for an enlightened teacher to check if one's views are right.

Xishan's Commentary

Such a work is not at all easy. One should continue to begin anew. Dao is like the great sea; the more one enters into it, the deeper it becomes. Never be satisfied with a tiny gain. If one does not find an enlightened teacher after one's realization, one's realization, which is as sweet as cream, will turn into poison.

Blowing Rock's Commentary

Zen Buddhism is not a search for an abstract truth. In other words, Zen is not something about which one theorizes or speculates. It is life itself. Zen person is really immersed in it. The interest of the enlightened person does not lie in searching for enlightenment. In other words, one's interest for enlightenment must be progressively diminished. Instead, one has to become more interested in seeking enlightened persons. Students of Dao should show interest in associating with people who are full of enlightenment. One should find a spiritual companion whom one can love and who also deserves one's love. In other words, one needs to make oneself loving. Then everything is easy.

Zen love, like all true love, is not merely between a person and the truth but also between a person and people who are full of truth. One loves the other, for one loves what the other loves. The real love, or Zen love, cannot be unrequited or narcissistic. If one wants to climb a tree, the other also climbs. This is the meaning of "sitting near a teacher." In sitting near a teacher, something inevitably rubs off on the other. Whatever has rubbed off on oneself can be passed on to others.

Case XXVI. Paying Attention To Your Deeds

A virtuous man of old said, "you regard dearly only what you have seen correctly, but you do not pay any attention to your deeds."

Xishan's Commentary

Master Yangshan answered master Weishan's question, "The forty volumes of *the Mahaparinirvana Sutra* are all the words of maras." This answer is Yangshan's correct view. Now Weishan answered Yangshan's question about deeds: "You regard dearly only what you have seen correctly, but you do not give any attention to your deeds." Here is the reason why one can talk about deeds only after one has begun to see things as they are. And thus one should first be enlightened in order for anyone to truly cultivate.

Blowing Rock's Commentary

Weishan (771–853 A. D.) studied Zen under master Baizhang. One winter night, he studied Zen late. Baizhang asked, "Is there any ember left in the brazier?" After checking the brazier, Weishan answered, "No ember at all, master!" Baizhang checked it for himself and found a tiny piece of charcoal still glowing in the ashes of the brazier. He said, "Is not this a fire?" At this, Weishan was enlightened.

Yangshan (814–890 A. D.) wanted to leave his home for Zen training. His father did not permit him to do that. Having cut off two of his fingers, finally he was permitted to leave home for attaining enlightenment at the age of seventeen. He met Weishan and asked him, "Where is the real place for Buddha to live?" Weishan answered, "Reflect upon a holy flame which is a mysterious principle of thoughtless thought: At the cul- de-sac of your thought, you will reach the place where matter and spirit are united and where action and principle are not two: This nondual place is the place for Buddha to be." At this answer, he was greatly enlightened. Later Weiyang School was named after the first part of their respective names.

The Mahaparinirvana Sutra contains the life and teachings of the Buddha and the meaning of nirvana. However, this *Sutra* does not help any one who is in direct union with one's own soul and thus has already attained Buddhahood. To many Buddhists, *the Mahaparinirvana Sutra* is thought of as enshrining a truth; they imagine themselves to possess that truth, and they try to define their own deeds in relation to that scripture. In that way, they limit their own lives and reduce their lives into a kind of abstraction. Their identities are really labels rather than a reality. Therefore, it is correct view to see that there are many limitations inherent in all the Buddhist scriptures: All the scriptures to some extent are finite, external to life, indecent, and uncreative. That is the reason why the Buddhist *Sutra* is characterized as the words of devils. In *the Diamond Sutra* the same point is expressed in a more unmistakable way:

> Buddha asked, "Subodai! What do you think about this: has the Buddha attained to perfect Enlightenment? Is there any Truth for him to teach?" Subodai answered, "According to the teaching of the Buddha, the World-Honoured One, there is nothing we can call perfect Enlightenment, neither is there any Truth for the Buddha to teach. Why not? Because we are not to adhere to the teaching of the Buddha, nor is it to be taught."

Correct view must liberate the human from all kinds of adherence to *the Sutras* to see things as they really are. The real place for Buddha to be is not in the scripture but the place where deeds are made by correct vision. Correct vision is "a holy flame which is a mysterious principle of thoughtless thought." "Thoughtless thought" comes into being only when thoughts are attached to nothing whatever. As the Zen scripture says, *Cherish thoughts that are dwelling on nothing whatever.*

An example of thoughtless thought is found in the following story, which has already been mentioned previously. A pupil approaches a Zen teacher and asks, "What is the highest teaching of Buddhism?" To this question, the teacher replies with another question, "Have you eaten your breakfast yet?" The pupil says, "Yes." The teacher retorts, "Then go and wash your bowls." That is all there is to Zen. Go and wash the bowls: nothing special. This is what Zen wishes students to see: One has to pay attention wholeheartedly to one's deeds whatever they are.

Case XXVII. Trusting In One's Mind

It is a wish that students of Dao should trust one's mind. One should neither humble oneself nor be proud of oneself.

Xishan's Commentary

The mind is so impartial that there is no distinction between an ordinary person and a sage. Although it is fundamentally so, some people are in fact ignorant and others are enlightened. And there are an ordinary person and an extraordinary person. When one realizes instantly the teachers' teaching that there is no difference between one's own self and Buddha, it is called sudden realization. Therefore, one should not humble oneself. It is the meaning of the sentence: "There is nothing from the beginning."

When one breaks off from one's old habits after one's realization and becomes a sage, it is called gradual cultivation. Therefore, one should not be proud of oneself. It is the meaning of the sentence, "Take care to keep it always clean."

Humility is a disease of the students who learn teachings of Buddha, while pride is a disease of the students who practice Zen. Students of Buddha's teachings do not trust in the mysterious law of Zen realization. Furthermore, they are so attached to the cleverness of teachings that they make a distinction between truth and falsity and that they do not cultivate contemplation and conduct. And thus they are merely counting other people's treasure, which does not make them any riches. Students of Zen do not trust in the good way of cultivating detachment through the teaching. They do not feel ashamed of their contaminated minds and their bad habits. And thus they are so proud of their thought about the law despite the shallowness of their learning. That is the reason why they speak arrogantly. Therefore, one, who has right learning to cultivate one's mind, neither humbles oneself nor is proud of oneself.

Xishan's Further Commentary

Neither to humble oneself nor to be proud of oneself has various implications: Generally speaking, the beginner's mind already contains the entire sea of fruits in its essence. And thus one should trust in nondual rank. However, looked at in specific detail, the fruits of a Bodhisattva reveal fifty-five different ranks sunken in the depth of the nondual essence.

Blowing Rock's Commentary

It is false humility that one does not trust in one's true self hidden deeply in one's individual self, which is nothing but Buddhahood. And thus, all beings are potentially Buddha. To realize the potential non-duality of self and Buddha is the beginner's mind. To keep the beginner's mind is true humility. Therefore, it is necessary for the beginner to actualize the potential non-duality. In other words, it is the responsibility of the students of Dao to make the implicit potentiality explicit. One who keeps this beginner's mind for the rest of one's life fears no fall.

The non-duality of self and Buddha can be revealed in fifty-five different ways; one barren wisdom, ten forms of belief, ten stations to stay, ten places to go, ten places to go around, four places to work hard, and ten forms of earth. It is a many splendorous thing which exhibits simultaneously many levels. It is pride of life that one tries to live one's own life superficially and monotonously. It is pride of place that one does not curb egoistic superficial pretension to one's true self, which is a cosmic dimension of life. Otherwise, as the saying goes, "Pride goes before a fall."

The person of Zen is to avoid these two extremes: false humility and pride. Whenever one of the two extremes captures one's life, one is in a state of eccentricity, that is, off-centeredness. This is the state of sin. Sin is separateness which comes from surrendering to the domination of one extreme of the two. Instead, one seeks to find the living center where there are no such extremes. Nevertheless, there is no need for the person of Zen to search for the center *externally*. And this awareness is the beginner's mind. And thus, one has to begin with and trust in one's mind. To search for the true center while not beginning with one's living self is likened to searching for a "rabbit's horn."

Case XXVIII. Being Ignorant Of Mind

While being ignorant of mind, cultivating Dao merely helps ignorance to increase.

Xishan's Commentary

How can one truly cultivate oneself without thorough awakening? Both awakening and cultivating are closely related to each other as both oil and fires go along with each other or as both eyes and feet mutually assist each other.

Blowing Rock's Commentary

The distance between cultivation and awakening must be annihilated. Zen is neither the championing of the cultivation nor the surrendering to awakening. It is the spiritual quest for the coincidence of the opposites, which is all in all. Zen person or the enlightened contain the opposites within oneself without any contradiction. To cultivate Dao while being ignorant of one's true self is to seek a rabbit's horn.

It is not like seeking a superficial golden mean, that is, a middle position in the sense that one tries to have a little of both the extremes. This kind of the golden mean is like a person who is trying to play tug of war, which has to be pulled in opposite directions. One goes this way for a while, and then one is pulled the other way. One's life is always vacillating. Perhaps the person who strives to take such a middle position is more sensible than either of the extremes. However, the life of that person is always oscillating rather than sure. Seen from this point of view, the awakened one realizes that one has got to have both *not as both, but in a kind of living unity*. Cultivation without awakening is blind. Awakening without cultivation is empty.

Case XXIX. The Kernel Of Cultivation

The kernel of cultivation is only to exhaust the thoughts of an ordinary person. There cannot be the separate knowledge of a sage.

Xishan's Commentary

When disease vanishes, one takes no more medicine. One is the very self before one was sick.

Blowing Rock's Commentary

Siddhartha Gautama did not seek any *special* kind of enlightenment after he had exhausted all kind of worldly passion, because the end of the worldly passions is the very content of enlightenment. The exhaustion of his worldly passion is the original face before he was born.

Enlightenment has to be everything or nothing. If the enlightenment is thought as just a special kind of human activity to which one devotes an hour or two a day, it is nothing. Religion can become one's primary interest in two different ways. The first is the traditional way of doing Buddhism. According to this way, there are two compartments of life: first of all, there is an ordinary form of human activity such as work, play, making friends, social participation, or political obligations in which ordinary persons are used to be engaged. Second, there is an extraordinary or religious form of human activity such as practicing the religious precepts or doing meditation in which monks are used to be engaged. To many Buddhists, the latter is most important. If one tries to make religion or Buddhism supreme in this way, the only way it can be supreme is by making all the ordinary activities subordinate to the sacred form of life. This effort to make one's religious activity supreme results in the depreciation of life's ordinary activities.

The other is the way of union with life in its totality. This way does not require a devaluation of one's ordinary life. When a religious practice becomes united with life, then it is no longer one department of life in competition with another department of life. The distinction between the ordinary and the extraordinary disappears. The distinction of the extraordinary from the ordinary is a mark of spiritual disease. For example, inferiority complex generated by an ordinary person is the same as superiority complex generated by a saint. To put it in another way, the essence of cultivation is not to attain a sage knowledge distinguished from an ordinary knowledge but simply to return to the one's original state of being by shaking off both inferiority complex and superiority complex. And thus one discovers the extraordinariness in the ordinary. For the enlightened, the ordinary thing takes on extraordinary significance. In a similar vein, Wordsworth points out that there is something very special about the nature of wisdom: To one who has returned to one's original state of health, wisdom is often nearer when the human stoops than when the human soars. His comments can be paraphrased to mean that what cannot be explained to an ordinary person or a child is not true wisdom: Or if it is true, it is not worth knowing. As an answer to his disciples' question, "Who is the greatest in the kingdom of heaven?" Jesus said: *Truly, I say to you, unless you turn and become like children, you will never enter the kingdom of heaven.*

Case XXX. Do Not Try To Abandon The Ordinary Mind

Do not try to abandon the ordinary mind. Just do not defile one's original nature. It is not true to search for the true Dharma.

Xishan's Commentary

Both abandoning and searching defile.

Blowing Rock's Commentary

If one abandons the ordinary mind, no one is going to replace it. Logically speaking, one becomes nobody. However, it is existentially impossible to be nobody, simply because somebody is always seeking to be nobody, who in turn is seeking to be somebody. This vicious cycle to abandon one's ordinary mind results from wrongly identifying true self with what is only an abstracted aspect of Dharma, that is, One Thing.

Enlightenment is just to *be*. The deepest enlightenment is not attainable through the attempt to model one's life on an external image of sagehood, which was enunciated apart from one's *own ordinary* self. Each individual is not merely the human race. Each is this concrete individual. If enlightenment is not custom-tailored to each individual measurement, it does not fit each individual. It will be either too tight for one's nature or too loose for one's frame. And thus it becomes abstraction. If enlightenment does not fit O'Hyun Park or any reader of this book, it is not worthy of attaining it.

The true Dharma is not something external to oneself. The true Dharma is the unknowable center of things. To see things as they really are is to open to the infinite mystery in things. Only in opening to the eternally unknown and unknowable center of life is there any living cultivation or growth. Real cultivation does not come from dealing with the known but from facing with the mystery of life. The living truth, which sets human free, is to be found only in the unknown center of things. The groping for that center is real seeking. All other seeking is perverse. And thus perverse seeking is to defile one's true nature.

Any other kind of seeking apart from seeking for the unknown center is merely playing a game called "hide and seek." That kind of seeking is what most of the people are inclined to play. Many behave like children who take an object such as a ball or an Easter egg to hide behind another object such as a piano or a tree. Then they go around looking for it. After seeking it everywhere in the fixed known area, they at last discover it to be behind the piano. This is not real seeking. It is just a hide and seek. Genuine seeking is to come only when one does not know what one is seeking for. It comes only when one does not know where to seek it and how to seek it or where to begin. Any other kind of seeking, that is external seeking, surely defiles one's original face. Whenever one expects an external answer to one's seeking, one defiles the purity of one's heart.

Case XXXI. No Arising Of Worldly Passions

Cutting off of worldly passions is the second vehicle. No arising of these passions is the great nirvana.

Xishan's Commentary

Cutting off consists of two elements: one who acts upon and the thing that is acted upon. No arising has neither activity nor passivity.

Blowing Rock's Commentary

The second vehicle is Hinayana Buddhism. The first vehicle is Mahayana Buddhism. Hinayana Buddhism is dualistic, while Mahayana Buddhism is non-dual. Zen Buddhism belongs to Mahayana Buddhism.

No arising of the worldly passion is the unconditional union with life. It means that a Zen student neither controls life nor is controlled by life. Life is not an object for one either to accept or to reject. Nor is it a tyrannical power to control one's life. Instead, one just lives life completely. Zen does not ask the student to put up a lot of resistance against life. It also does not ask him/her to yield to it. Unconditional union with life is absolute reconciliation with life. It is neither activity nor passivity. It is non-duality between passivity and activity. That is no arising of worldly passions. It means that the enlightened person does what can be done, when it can be done. And the person lets the rest go and *accepts* the whole thing just as it is.

Seen from this point of view, to the enlightened who lives the unconditional union with life, life itself is not a problem. *Therefore do not worry about tomorrow, for tomorrow will worry about itself. Each day has enough trouble of its own.* There are plenty of specific problems, but life itself is no longer problematic. Seen from this point of view, the life of the enlightened is like the life of animals. For example, one can learn a great deal from watching how animals handle the problem of fleas. When the fleas bite, they just scratch. They do not curse God. They do not consider the problem of why God created fleas. There is no problem of evil in theology for them. It is very simple, that is, simply profound or profoundly simple: one bites, the other scratches. One has no grievances against life itself.

Case XXXII. Emptying Oneself

One should empty oneself to mirror itself. One should trust that not a single thought caused by karma arises in reality, although it appears to arise.

Xishan's Commentary

This merely explains the arising of one's own nature.

Blowing Rock's Commentary

T. S. Eliot said in his poem, *The Hollow Men:*

We are the hollow men
We are the stuffed men
Leaning together
headpiece filled with straw. Alas!
Our dried voices, when
We whisper together
Are quiet and meaningless
As wind in dry grass
Or rats' feet over broken glass
In our dry cellar

One is a hollow person, because one is filled with unnecessary stuffs. One needs to empty them. Otherwise, one's mind smeared with stuffs causes the production of the world of multiplicity, which will be subject to the law of causation.

In reality, there is neither appearance nor disappearance. As Huineng said, "There is nothing from the beginning." According to him, both appearance and disappearance are the result of ignorance. For example, with the absence of light, a person may mistake a piece of rope lying on the ground for a snake. And consequently one may run away from it, frightened and trembling. Another person may tell the other, "Do not be afraid, it is not a snake but only a rope." And then one may dismiss the fear caused by the imagined snake. The appearance and following disappearance of one's mistaken thought makes no difference whatever in the rope itself. Likewise, appearance and disappearance of one thought are merely the result of spiritual ignorance. The difference between them is in name only. It is senseless to insist on the difference between arising and no-arising. *The Diamond sutra* says:

> All things that appear in the world are ephemeral. If one views all things that appear as never having appeared, then one will realize one's true self.

Case XXXIII. The Place Of Arising Is Originally Empty

Observe carefully the fact that killing, stealing, lusting, and lying all arise from one mind. As the place of arising is originally empty, what is there to be cut off again?

Xishan's Commentary

It explains one's own nature and its phenomena as well. *The Sutra* says, "To destroy ignorance is not to give rise to a single thought." It also says, "Awake, whenever a thought arises."

Blowing Rock's Commentary

In the Upanishads, through which a spirit of Zen flows, one of the most beautiful metaphors is found. There is a person who rides in one's chariot driven by horses. Having given over authority for the journey to one's charioteer, one is totally free to sit serenely and enjoy the passing landscape. In this story lies a metaphor of the attitude of Zen. Metaphorically speaking, the chariot is human body. The road stands for sense objects. The horses that pull the chariot are senses themselves. The reins are human mind that disciplines the senses. The driver is human soul which controls the mind. However, the master of the chariot who delegates full authority to the driver and needs to lift not a single finger is one's true self, that is, one's spirit.

Likewise, if Zen students carefully observe both the phenomena of the world and their minds, they are able to build up the eightfold path (right belief, right purpose, right speech, right conduct, right livelihood, right effort, right mindfulness, and right meditation). One becomes capable of observing things with a calm detachment. As one might let one's fart disappear in the wind or as the sun that shines on the universe is unconcerned with what goes on within it, so one as the witness watches what goes on in the universe, this world, and the limit of empirical self. And one does everything in stride.

Case XXXIV. Nothing To Cultivate

Whenever one understands the nature of illusion, one has already got rid of it. One needs not to resort to any other means. Whenever one is rid of illusion, one has already been awakened. Furthermore, there is nothing for one to cultivate.

Xishan's Commentary

One's mind is the magician of illusion. One's body is the castle of illusion. The world is the clothes of illusion. Both name and form are the food of illusion. Moreover, arising of mind, moving of thought, speaking of falsehood and speaking of truth are all illusions. Ignorance like a phantasmagoria without beginning, arises from the mind. Since every phantasm is like a flower in the sky, so the absence of a phantasm is nothing but the non-arising place. One, who is sick in the dream, may seek a doctor. Awakening from the dream, one does not need any resort to medical treatment. It is likewise, when one realizes all things as illusions.

Blowing Rock's Commentary

In Hinduism, the word "magic" comes from the same root as "maya." Maya means illusion, which deceives humans by giving a false impression or idea. It plays tricks on humans to be attached to "seeming" rather than "being." A person lying sick in one's dream remains a healthy person even while one is mistaken for a patient. However, whenever one realizes that all things are illusions, one can learn to play along with them. It is as if an actor plays one's given role on the stage, whatever one's role may be. Likewise, thinking, doing, speaking, and willing in one's everyday life continue, but one does not take them too seriously. And that is the life of Zen. It is like playing a game, which has no truth outside the game. Each game is its own point. It is fun in itself. It is no more or no less. Speaking of falsehood, for example, is no less true and no more symbolic than speaking of truth. One can lie in the speaking of truth just as much as in the speaking of falsehood.

More than anything else found in *the Bible*, Jesus went to the bathroom. This action was no less true and no more secular than the breaking of bread and drinking of grape juice at the holy sacrament.

There is no real distinction between secular and sacred. Thinking makes it so. What is good to one can be bad to the other. One's own food can be poisonous to the other. Real goodness is not just the suppression of badness. Realizing this, one no longer needs to cultivate one's goodness by suppressing one's badness. It is an impossible task to try to be good. No matter how long one tries to be good in this way, but one remains to be bad. Instead of being this or that, one needs just to be. Just to be is the non-arising place where the locus of authenticity lies. In other words, being just so is good in itself. It is so neither because it can be contrasted to this nor because it can be compared with that. It is so because it is just what it is. "There is nothing left for one to cultivate."

Case XXXV. Seeing A Flower In The Sky

The unenlightened people absurdly see the cycle of life-death and nirvana from the non-arising place. It is likened to seeing a flower in the sky, which seems to appear and disappear.

Xishan's Commentary

One's original nature has nothing to be born from itself, so there is neither the cycle of life-death nor nirvana. From the beginning, there is not anything in the sky. So there is neither appearance nor disappearance. Seeing the cycle of life-death is like seeing a flower appearing in the sky. Seeing nirvana is like seeing a flower disappearing from the sky. In true reality, appearance is disappearance, there is no need to argue about the two views. As it is said in the *Sijijing*, "The coming of all the Buddhas into the world is not to take living beings away but only to take away the two views of both the cycle of life-death and nirvana."

Blowing Rock's Commentary

In Buddhism, the endless cycle of life and death is called samsara, which makes human history possible. History records the appearance and disappearance of human events. Anything that has a history is samsara. The endless cycle of history, however, arises within the non-arising place. And thus, there is no real distinction between the cycle and nirvana. Nirvana is not just a goal to be reached outside of samsara. Enlightenment, that is, entrance into nirvana, is not just an end result to be achieved by certain means found in samsara. If the means is not real, how can they lead to nirvana as a goal? If the cycle of life-death is separated from nirvana, how will one reach the goal. In Zen, one cannot separate samsara and nirvana. Samsara can be likened to the waxing of the moon. Nirvana can be likened to the waning of the moon. The waxing and waning of the moon do not affect the essence of the moon. Seen from the essence of the moon, the waxing is the waning. There is no real difference between the two.

Many sincere Buddhists may be persuaded that one is only looking for the proper means and that once one finds them, one will apply oneself diligently to those means until they bring oneself to the goal which is totally different from the means. But to envisage the religious quest in this way is to make a false separation between means and end, which leads to a false separation between samsara and nirvana. Going to nirvana is not half the fun. In Zen, getting there is all the fun. In fact, one never gets there. In fact, there is no place to go. The non-arising place is where the cycle of life-death, nirvana, and enlightenment are ultimately one.

Enlightenment is to see things as they really are. The appropriate reason for the coming of Buddhas into the world is not to take the living beings away out of the endless cycle of life-death or take them into nirvana. It is to let them see things exactly as they are by taking away the two lopsided views.

The enlightened seek to replace two false assumptions made out of the two views. First of all, it is false assumption that enlightenment can be bestowed from the other. The enlightened see that enlightened view cannot be given from the outside or passively received from within. It must be won. Second, it is false assumption that there is truth in the singular totally apart from truths in the plural. The enlightened, however, see that truths in the plural and truth in the singular are two names of the non-arising place. Until and unless this is made real, neither truth in the singular nor truths have any real meaning. The non-arising place is an ontological place where union of the two opposites takes place. It is the *summum bonum*. There is no right higher than that of the non-arising place. The non-arising place has no obligation to take sides with any one of them. It is both truth in the singular and truths in the plural to fashion themselves to the non-arising place.

Case XXXVI. The Bodhisattvas' Help

Although it could be said that the Bodhisattvas took living beings into nirvana, no living beings in reality attained nirvana.

Xishan's Commentary

The Bodhisattvas only and devotedly think of living beings. To understand that the nature of thinking is empty is to liberate them. Whenever thought is emptied and mind is pacified, there are no living beings left to attain nirvana. The above passage deals with trust and liberation.

Blowing Rock's Commentary

The Bodhisattvas are those who are spiritually liberated and yet refuse to enter nirvana or to be distinguished from the living beings. Instead, they wholly help them to attain spiritual liberation without taking them into nirvana. Their help is just to free them from the false view that nirvana is different from samsara. Seen from their point of view, there is no real distinction between the Bodhisattvas who save and the living beings who are in dire need of salvation.

Spiritual freedom has nothing to do either with rational freedom or with impulsive freedom. The Bodhisattvas are not governing themselves in the light of rational principles. Nor are they governed by impulses which happen to be momentarily uppermost in themselves. The Bodhisattvas are neither consenting rationally to what one has to do nor doing what they feel like doing. Freedom generated by the Bodhisattvas is neither of these, but perfect integrity in which what they have to do and what they feel like doing are one and the same thing.

In other words, perfect integrity does not entail a victory of one part of the person over the other. It is the freedom of the whole person to act as a whole. It is the absence of inner conflict and restraint. Therefore, it is the center of life itself for all the radii. This living center is the non-arising place where the Bodhisattvas stand and comprehend all the radii together.

Anything that is centered is contagious to all the radii. Spiritual freedom is no exception. In other words, contagious freedom simply rubs off on the living beings and frees them from all kinds of dualistic view imprinted in their minds; nirvana and samsara, the ordinary and the extraordinary, freedom and bondage, etc. In other words, the Bodhisattvas help others without helping them objectively. Therefore, *The Diamond Sutra* said: "Although it could be said that the Bodhisattvas saved a lot of living beings, in actual fact there is no one left to receive the salvation." In actual fact, nirvana and samsara are not to be separated. From the moment they are enlightened to the moment they die, they have samsara-nirvana, a unity of mental and physical changes which at no time can be called nirvana and at no time samsara, but which at every point is *both*. Therefore, life lived by a Bodhisattva really means what is called "samsara-nirvana." Death means *no more* samsara-nirvana.

Case XXXVII. The Principles And The Habits

Although one can realize the principle abruptly, one cannot get rid of the habits suddenly.

Xishan's Commentary

Bodhisattva Wenshu reached the heavenly truth, while Bodhisattva Puxian explained the moral law of causation. Awakening is like a flash of lightning, while deeds are like a baby. The following passage deals with both cultivation and realization.

Blowing Rock's Commentary

Bodhisattvas are personified aspects of Buddha's nature. Bodhisattva Wenshu represents the Buddha's wisdom. Bodhisattva Puxian represents the Buddha's love. Since all human beings are originally Buddha, his wisdom and love are originally in human beings. Therefore, it can be said that Wenshu is the wisdom within, while Puxian is the love within.

Although awakening is sudden like a flash of lightning, to do things properly is the most difficult thing in the world. Baijuyi (772–846), the minister of a district in China, said to Zen master Daolin, "You are in a very dangerous place!" The master said, "You are in a more dangerous one." Baijuyi said, "What is dangerous about being in charge of this province?" Daolin said, "How can you say you are not in danger when your passions are burning like fire, and you can't stop worrying about this and that?" Baijuyi then asked, "What is the essence of Buddhism?" Daolin answered, "Not to do any evil, just purify oneself." Baijuyi said, "Any child of three knows this." Daolin said, "That is so, but even a man of eighty cannot do it."

The essence of Zen is to purify oneself. To purify oneself is to wholeheartedly do anything at all in any conceivable circumstances. That is all Zen is: Do eat when one is hungry, sleep when one is tired. Many people cannot get rid of the habit to eat, when they are not hungry. Many times, they are pulled by eating disorder. Many people have the habit to be awake, when they are tired. Furthermore, they try to sleep with sleeping pills. Sometimes, these kinds of habits make people appear like intruders. In other words, their own deeds are in direct opposition to their own selves.

On the other hand, the enlightened who purifies oneself must be able, that is, wholeheartedly willing, to do anything on any occasion whatever. In other words, one must learn to like whatever one does, instead of doing what one likes to do. Each act, each thought, and each emotion are to be expressed with the whole and indivisible mind-body in totality. That is all. As Zen saying goes, *When you walk, just walk. If you sit, just sit; but don't wobble, whatever you do.* Whenever one attains this state of union, it is perfectly alright to talk *about* Zen.

When one attains such a wholeheartedness, one is released from the cycle of cause-and-effect. *Whoever finds his life will lose it, and whoever loses his life for my sake will find it.* All forms of life —past, present, and future—are in God's hands; whether one's life continues or it fizzles out, one is able to say "Thank God!" One's life without judgement or without weighing is the union of wisdom and love, that is, the unconditional union with life itself. As *the Bible* says, *love delights in the wisdom (the truth).*

Case XXXVIII. Mara's Way

Doing Zen while desiring for indulgence of sex is like boiling sands to make rice. Practicing Zen while killing is like shouting with one's own ear blocked. Doing Zen while stealing is like trying to fill a leaky bowl. Doing Zen while lying is like making incense with dung. No matter how much knowledge these things possess, they merely build mara's way.

Xishan's Commentary

This explains the three rules of cultivation. Hinayana keeps laws as its precept. That is the reason why it rules the tips in a general way. Mahayana keeps the mind as its precept. That is the reason why it breaks off the roots in detail. Therefore, the precept in accordance with the laws keeps the body from doing wrong. The precept of the mind keeps thoughts from doing wrong.

Desiring for indulgence of sex severs one from purity. Killing severs one from love. Stealing severs one from felicity and virtue. Lying severs one from truth. Although one may attain the six divine tricks through manyfold knowledge of Zen, unless one severs oneself from killing, stealing, desiring for indulgence of sex and lying, one will surely fall into the way of mara. And, therefore, one will eternally lose the right way of Bodhi.

Since these four precepts are the source of all precepts, one should make special attention to them so that one should not commit these things even in one's own thoughts. Not to think is called the precept. The absence of thought is called contemplation. Not to be foolish is called wisdom. In other words, the precept is to catch a thief. Contemplation is to bind the thief. Wisdom is to kill the thief. Furthermore, the vessel of the precept must be complete and strong so that it will be cleanly filled with the water of contemplation. Accordingly, the moon of wisdom will arise.

These three methods of cultivation are essentials of all the dharmas. One should give special attention to them, lest any one of them should be leaky. How could there be a reckless Buddha on the mount Gijihakuta? How could there be a patriarch telling a lie in the school of Xiaolin?

Blowing Rock's Commentary

One who has a wall-eyed vision has a lopsided view: One eye is on the Zen practice, while the other eye is on the objective world. The split between Zen and ordinary life is an illusory difference that Zen seeks to break down. Zen is not any item in life. It is just life itself creatively lived.

Ego is essentially an amalgamation of three basic ingredients of desire: lust, grasping, and greed. Such an amalgamated ego is always conscious of itself. Such an ego-centered consciousness inevitably produces threefold poisonous aversion: anger, fear, and hatred. Furthermore, such an ego is ignorant of the truth that the ego-centered consciousness of goodness as over against badness is the root of all problems.

The real mark of Zen is that it is not conscious of itself. It is forgetful of itself. It is no longer self-conscious. Zen is not a good commodity that one consciously carries around in oneself.

The purpose of doing Zen, therefore, is neither to stay in the ego's goodness nor to share egoistic goodness with others. It is to transcend both goodness and badness. In other words, it is beyond what ego calls "good" or "evil," not partly both. Ego's Zen may confer the six divine tricks on people: 1) It may cause people to be transfigured. 2) One may see things far away. 3) One may hear every sort of sound. 4) One may penetrate into others' minds and know their thoughts. 5) One may know lives of living beings, past, present, and future. 6) One may end all kinds of suffering. Insofar as ego is not transcended, all these six tricks lead to the way of mara (the evil one).

Ego-centered consciousness, however, must be transformed by three methods of cultivation. First, one keeps the body from wrong doing. Second, one practices not to remember or not to think in terms of dualism of good and bad. Third, one continues to practice "no-thinking" until one is forgetful of one's ego, whose nature is to make discrimination between good and bad. To practice no-thinking is called "wisdom." For example, Bodhidharma meditated at the Xiaolin temple for nine years to attain forgetfulness of his ego. In his forgetfulness, he was yet able to attend to each step as it came. In other words, he did not make any mistake in wherever he treaded. He had only the perfect indivisible oneness with nature, in which his forgetfulness becomes cosmic consciousness.

Case XXXIX. Virtue

People without virtue neither rely upon the Buddha's precepts nor look after the threefold action. Doing things recklessly and idling away their time, they indulge in despising, disputing, and quarreling with others.

Xishan's Commentary

If the mind-precept is broken, a hundred faults arise simultaneously.

Xishan's Further Commentary

Students should well keep in mind that a crowd of maras lead people astray in the end of the world and obstruct the right dharma.

Blowing Rock's Commentary

Virtue comes from wisdom, which is neither a knowledge nor an information. Both knowledges and informations come from many parts of oneself; either the five senses or reason. These kinds of things must come from the intellectual separation of mind and body. "The threefold action" is an action made by either one's body, one's lip, or one's head. Virtue must come from one's total self, that is, the unity of one's physical action and one's word and one's thought. In other words, virtue comes into being, whenever any part of oneself is sponsored, authored, or authorized by one's total being. If the purpose of one's life is to look after the threefold action, that is, the non-duality of bodily action and word and thought, any thing will suffice at any time in any place.

When Confucius was asked about two Chinese officials who gave up the throne and their lives rather than do wrong, "Had they any regrets?" Confucius answered, "They sought for virtue; they got virtue: what was there for them to regret?"

Knowledges or informations are gained from a position, which means a pose or a posturing. To identify oneself only in terms of one's own position is to be anchored in abstractions, which are the plurality of maras. Real identity is of spirit, and so far as one is afraid to rely upon the Buddha's precepts whose essence is nothing but the mind-precept, one seeks a false identity through one of many labels or positions. That is the reason why one despises, disputes, and quarrels with others. Since one's identity is not real, one is always in peril of being exposed. So there is a fearfulness and a fanaticism based on hatred lurking in the background of every position. Virtue is never defensive; it never feels opposed or threatened. A truly virtuous person has nothing to defend, because one is not grasping onto anything which might be torn out of one's hands. One has only one's own life to live, one's own reality to communicate. As Huineng said, *There is nothing to argue about here, every argument is sure to go against the intent of it.* One cannot argue with a real smile, or with a true handshake. One cannot argue with a person who works truly. One can argue only with ideas, knowledges, or informations, that is, with partialities or abstractions. Virtue like reality is not open to argument; it is not grasped via arguments. Whenever wisdom, that is, the mind-precept, is broken, all the rest of faults come into being.

Case XL. The Precepts

If one does not practice the precepts, one cannot be born even as a mean fox who gets the mange; how in the world can one expect to attain the undefiled fruit of Bodhi!?

Xishan's Commentary

If one respects the precepts as if one serves the Buddha, it will be just like being with Buddha. One should follow the examples of monks found in "the grass-bound monk" and "the goose and the jewel."

Blowing Rock's Commentary

A mean fox has a skin disease that causes loss of hair. Without its hair, a neckerchief cannot be made. Furthermore, the fox has a certain power of cunning that other animals do not have: It is clever in deceiving and sly in getting what it wants. The fox here is the symbol of its uselessness and its double personality.

When the Buddha was about to enter nirvana, his disciples asked him, "Who will be our teacher?" The Buddha answered, "Take my teachings as your teacher." The respecting of Buddha's precepts is the ushering of the Buddha's presence. When one keeps the precepts, the Buddha is in the act of keeping the precepts.

"The grass-bound monk" is a story about a monk who traveled along a field in India. He was met by a thief. The thief took the monk's clothes and tied him to grasses. Since he had vowed not to injure any living being, including the grasses, he waited for a passer-by to untie him. At last, a king, who came out hunting, passed by him, and released him from the grasses. Moved by his practice of the vow, the king gave up hunting and became a Buddhist.

"The Goose and the Jewel" is also a story about a monk who visited a family to beg for some food. At that time, the head of the family was polishing a jewel ordered by a king. When the householder left the place for a while, a goose came by and swallowed the jewel. The monk saw the goose swallowing it, however, he kept his mouth shut, because his telling of the truth might cause the goose to be killed. Having found out that the jewel was missing, the householder considered the monk a thief and abused him. The monk's body was bleeding and the ground was stained with blood. The goose came along and started to eat the blood dropped on the ground. In a fit of anger, the householder kicked the goose and killed it. At last, the monk opened his mouth, saying, "The goose swallowed it."

Case XLI. Greed And Lust

If one wants to free oneself from the cycle of life-death, first of all, one should end greed and get rid of desire for indulgence of sex.

Xishan's Commentary

Sexual love is the root of transmigration. The desire for indulgence of sex is the cause to receive a body. As Buddha said, "If one does not get rid oneself of voluptuous mind, one cannot get out of the dust." Furthermore he said, "Once lust gets entangled with oneself, it packs oneself off to the gate of sin." The desire for indulgence of sex means a blaze of one's fervent sexual desire.

Blowing Rock's Commentary

People get hooked to things. And that is the real problem described in this case. A Korean Zen master, Won Hyo, said, "The desire for indulgence of sex is like a porcupine who crawls into a rat's hole." It is very easy to go into, but utterly impossible to back out. It does not matter how hard one tries. In this way, people create a new karma through their attachment-actions. If anyone is not attached to anything, then there is freedom from the dust of the world. The dust consists of worldly pleasures. Worldly pleasures are the result of being attached to things in the world.

It is like falling in love with someone. Falling-in-love-with is diametrically opposite to living union or genuine love. During the stage of falling in love, one knows the fact that one is in love. One knows the fact that one is lucky. One knows the fact that worldly pleasures are delicious and wonderful. What is wrong with it? It is wrong, because this state of awareness is really a self-centered state of knowledge. One is congratulating oneself on the wonderful thing that has happened to oneself. This self-congratulation is the root of egoism. One's beloved is merely an object of one's love. One does not participate in a mutual love relationship. Instead, one consciously or unconsciously controls or manipulates the other. Sex without genuine love is a wrong thing.

Case XLII. Wisdom

Wisdom, that is unhindered and pure, comes from Zen.

Xishan's Commentary

To reach the sage by transcending the ordinary; to undress while sitting; to die while standing are all the power of Zen. Therefore, a sage said, "if one seeks the holy way, there is no other way than this."

Blowing Rock's Commentary

When one's meditation is real, one is free of the cycle of life-and-death to which the ordinary is subject. It does not mean that one goes out of the cycle. It means that one enters into the cycle to live life completely. One of the most distressing things about people today is that one sees so few among the middle-aged and elderly whose faces reveal the real union with life. So many faces show a grievance that they have been cheated. They reveal a feeling that they did not get what they wanted out of life. This indicates that current civilization, despite the many things it gives them, somehow has not produced in them the right relationship with life.

The real touchstone of Zen meditation is the manner in which Zen people confront death, which can never be taken away from humans. Only when one's meditation is complete, can one say with Job, *Yea though God slays me, yet will I trust in Him*. For what does one trust God? It is just to slay one's own self. That is all. If anyone trusts God for something else, that is not absolute trust. To the life of Zen, everything that has to happen, even death, is just as it should be. Such a Zen meditation has not to resort to the props of faith in an endless cycle of life or in nirvana. Zen life perfectly embraces whatever God offers. That is unobstructed and pure wisdom.

Case XLIII. True Samadhi

If one's mind resides in samadhi, one is able to know clearly all the worldly affairs which appear and disappear.

Xishan's Commentary

Tiny dust particles lightly dance in the sunlight shining through a window. All kinds of images are clearly reflected in the clear calm water.

Blowing Rock's Commentary

Usually, samadhi means an unmoved state of mind. When one's mind moves, one's life is oscillating. An oscillating life is the life of thinking based on either/or logic. In this state, all things are divided into opposites: like and dislike, A and not A. One is forced to choose one object as over against the other. One may choose good and avoid bad, but one never succeeds. One's mind continually oscillates between opposites. For example, one may try to get rid of the tiny dust particles by obsessively cleaning the room. Life here is full of a struggle. One may take the struggle very seriously. One may wrestle continually with the dust particles. However, one never wins over the war, although one may win the battle. The struggle is ineradicable.

When one is aware of the impossibility to eradicate the struggle, one may try to dwell in some sorts of absorption in whatever one is doing. And one may be capable of seeing things with a stoic serenity: Although all things have different names and forms, they are of the same substance; for example, the Pacific Ocean is not the Atlantic Ocean; but both of them are of the same substance, that is, water: Furthermore, one may develop an argument that nothing is either good or bad and that thinking makes it so or not so. Hence one may come to thinking that struggle for life is not necessary: And therefore, one becomes resigned. Many people think that a certain amount of resignation is supposed to be a symptom of spiritual maturity. However, resignation is not the final goal of true samadhi. It is still an attachment-thinking that everything is the same. In other words, it is the product of very logical thinking that doing is not doing or that living is dying.

When one comes to realization that one's mind is not satisfied with the life of resignation, one's mind may enter the area of freedom where one may be able to freely create some kinds of unusual activity. If one wants to project light on the wall of a room, one can do that. If one wants death, one has death. Or one may cause a Buddha statue to cry. Although such worlds are very attractive for one to live, one should not try to stay there. One must transcend these worlds of miracle or magic in order to enter true samadhi, that is, Zen.

When one's mind enters true samadhi, one's mind just lets the tiny particles dance in the room and lets all images reflected in one's pure mind. All things are just as they are. The truth is just like this. There is no attachment to anything, including non-attachment. The tiny dust particles are no longer to bother one's mind, although one may be allergic to it. One's attitude toward the dust is not the same as before true samadhi. One does not need to be detached from them or to be oblivious of them. The tiny dust particles are just tiny dust particles, no more and no less. In other words, a dust particle is just a matter in its place like a diamond or a chunk of cloud. All kinds of images are clearly reflected in the clear clam water. An image is an image, no more and no less. In other words, the image of Buddha is just an image in its place like an image of any human being. Zen person simply let them be as they really are. Zen, that is, true samadhi, aims at helping one awaken one's mind without fixing it anywhere.

Case XLIV. Non-arising Mind

When mind in the midst of the worldly affairs does not wobble, it is called non-arising. Non-arising is called no thought. No thought is called spiritual freedom.

Xishan's Commentary

One may choose any one from the three: precepts, concentration, and wisdom, the other two follows. They are not three separate things.

Blowing Rock's Commentary

Religious precepts, unlike legal precepts, should not be external to inner concentration and genuine wisdom. Precepts without concentration are doctrinaire. Without wisdom, precepts can be misused. Likewise, concentration without precepts is blindly self-indulgent. Without wisdom, concentration is spooky or magical. Furthermore, wisdom without precepts is vague. Wisdom without concentration is barren.

In these circumstances, one may come to the conclusion that the truth consists of combining these three separate things, and that the reality exists in trying to have a little of these three entities. To have a little of each of the three is more sensible perhaps than choosing of the three. Nevertheless, it is wrong to think that one has to have the three in a kind of sandwich— a triple-layered sandwich.

One has to have the three not as three, but in some kind of living unity, the triunity. Zen means finding that living unity where one is not pulled by these three separate elements in different directions.

Zen becomes a search for the living center of life in which one finds something comprehensive or inclusive or satisfying. In this sense, Zen provides a bird's eye view in replacement of a worm's eye view. This living center, that is, the triunity, is the aim of Zen students. The person of the triunity can never be doctrinaire. To the extent that one is religious, one will never try to put the truth in some kind of capsule and say, "Here it is" or "There it is," because what is living cannot be encapsulated. Whenever one encapsulates life, it dies. The aim of Zen students is to find this living spirit in every situation, to live with it, and to be guided by it in whatever one is doing. Spirit used here is not some kind of gassy or shadowy figure. Students of Dao never rest on anything, whether they are precepts, concentration, or wisdom. The life of Zen is not a life based on any partisan or lopsided view. The triune life is the life of well-rounded personality, that is, the life which stems directly from that absolute source in relation to which all views are abstractions. Zen is wholeheartedly entering into union with the triune life by way of keeping the religious precepts wisely.

Case XLV. One Does Not Attain Nirvana

It is not truth that one attains nirvana by cultivating Dao. True nirvana is to understand that the mind is originally still. Thus it is said, "From the beginning, all things are nirvana as they are."

Xishan's Commentary

No one can see one's own eyes. If one does, one is deluded. Therefore, Bodhisattva Miaoshou thought aloud, while Bodhisattva Jingming was silent. The following cases will deal with deeds in detail.

Blowing Rock's Commentary

Nirvana is reality, truth, beauty, or God. Nirvana is not just a goal. It is not just an end result to be achieved by certain steps or means. If the means are not real, how can they lead to nirvana as a goal? If the means are false or contrived, how will they ever produce truth, naturalness, or freedom? In Zen, one cannot separate the means and the ends.

If the meaning of life, that is, the kingdom of heaven, is separated from life here and now, then life itself becomes meaningless. One inevitably abandons life and gives oneself to the meaning. If the truth of life is something different from, beyond, or over and above life itself, then life itself in this world is devoid of truth. As soon as one makes explicit the life-denying implications of such divorce between nirvana and samsara, one realizes how impossible it is to make such a separation. Cultivation of Dao based upon separation between means and ends merely leads one to impossibility. And yet most people in most religions operate on the assumption that such a separation actually reflects the ultimate nature of things. They believe that there is something on the other shore called nirvana or Buddha or reality or the kingdom of heaven or the meaning of life and something on this shore called the individual and one's ordinary life.

It is most needful to realize that in relation to living truth there are no means separated from life. Nirvana is not attained by cultivating means but through giving oneself utterly to one's life. The more one learns to give oneself, the more one enters into the reality of life.

Therefore, one must not look to a conference on religion and psychology to relieve one of the tasks of living one's own life. There are many who look to psychology or psychotherapy or to spiritual writings for answers. This is all right up to a point, but pushed too far it becomes an escape from oneself, that is, from one's own reality. If one keeps asking, "*How* shall I do it?" one is not meeting one's own life situation. One's own life can teach one *how* it is to be lived. If one turns to psychology or to religion because one is afraid to face one's own life, to sweat and to toil and shed tears and to learn to love in the context of one's own existential situation, then psychology and religion become obstacles to reality.

Since this is what happens to most people, it can perhaps be said paradoxically that the greatest obstacle to religion is religion, and the greatest obstacle to self-understanding is psychology. One must never approach these as forms of knowledge, which will exempt one from the necessity of actually living and learning from life itself.

Jingming is also known as Vimalakirti. When he was confined to his bed, many monks came to pay a sympathetic visit. Each one of them started to talk about the non-dual truth. Miaoshou, who is also known as Manjusri, *said*, "It cannot be expressed in words." In this way, he thought aloud about silence. Jingming just sat in his bed without uttering any word. All other monks praised Jingming, because he *explained* the non-dual truth by simply being silent.

Silence may betoken two opposite states of mind. Sometimes one is reduced to silence through ignorance or lack of an answer. It can be likened to a situation where a student is silent in the face of a teacher's questioning. Sometimes one is reduced to silence not by virtue of any dearth of knowledge but from just the opposite cause, namely, from the impossibility of giving voice to something so full and rich that it defies all description. If one has met a person casually, it may not be too difficult to say that the person is *this* kind of person or *that*. Suppose one has lived with someone for fifty years and is asked what kind of person is one's husband or one's wife. How can one answer the question? The more abstract our relationship, the more easily one can sum up the person or the situation in a verbal description. However, the more richly concrete the relationship, the more deeply involved one is, the closer to the living reality, the more difficult it is to compress the experience into words. Even as one speaks, one feels the gap between what one says and the reality one experiences.

Case XLVI. True Charity

When a poor person comes to beg, give one's possession within limits. True charity is to relish suffering of the other as one's own.

Xishan's Commentary

Self and other are not two bodies but one. It is our livelihood that we come empty-handed and leave empty-handed.

Blowing Rock's Commentary

If one lives the Zen life, that is, the religious life, one should not let anything exist between self and other. Whenever one does not live the life of Zen, each individual seems to have two sets of interests. There appears to be an unbridgeable gulf between the two. On the one hand, self is just I. I am concerned about my rights, my happiness, my property, my pleasures, or my opinion. On the other hand, self is not just I. I am also my family, my friends, my country, and all humankind eventually.

If one thinks that one can live just for oneself, one soon finds that one suffocates and loses the meaning of life. On the other hand, if one thinks that one can live just for the other, one shall soon find that it is just as impossible as to live only for one's own self. The fact is that one cannot be self-sacrificing all the time. And one cannot be just selfish or self-concerned all the time. That is the reason why one just gives one's possessions *within limits*. One cannot live just for oneself and one cannot just live for the other. Therefore, what does one do? Hillel said, "If I am not for myself, who is going to be for me?" "And if I live only for myself, what do I have out of life?"

This kind of problem only arises, because one exists somehow out of life and then one has to choose between self and other. Whenever there is a separation between I and Thou, that is an indication that one is not living from the true center of life. In other words, it is a symptom that one's relationship is not one of love, which casts out all fear. When one's relationship to other is one of loving union, one is not just outside the other, but in other, one with other; then the problem of selfish interest versus other's interest cannot arise. Other's interest is one's own interest, and one's own interest is other's interest. Whenever one lives the life of love, or when one is established in the ultimate non-duality of life, or whenever one is living from the divine center, which embraces both self and other, there is no dualism of self and other. So there is non-duality between one's self and others.

Whenever one lives the Zen life, one never lets one's possessions exist between self and other. Possessions that one can give others within limits are threefold; material possessions such as money, food, drink, clothes or shelter; spiritual possessions such as knowledge or wisdom; and virtuous possessions such as the keeping of the precepts. All these possessions, like money in their essence, are not to be saved but to be current. In other words, Zen person regards these things not as something to be possessed but as something to be passed on. In this way, true charity can be based upon not what people want but what people need.

Case XLVII. Not To Get Angry

Even though someone comes to hurt, one should take care of one's own mind not to get angry or to resent. When one thought causes oneself to get angry, the gate of one million barriers opens.

Xishan's Commentary

Although worldly passions are boundless, anger is worst. It is said in *the Nirvana Sutra*, "Be nonchalant either to injury made by spear and knife or to treatment made by perfume and medicine." Getting angry is likened to a bolt of lightning from the white clouds.

Blowing Rock's Commentary

Worldly passions in Buddhism are generated by desire, anger, and ignorance. Among these three, anger is worst. Anger is very closely related to hatred and fear. Anger comes into being, whenever one is forced or has to make one's *choice*. Making choice is basically *either/or,* which is wrongly believed to be the road to heaven. However, the life of Zen is *both/and*, which leads to heaven. If this matter of making choice is right, Zen is planting one's footsteps firmly on the road to hell. It is because Zen is suggesting that peace of soul can never ensue from making choice, which results in becoming angry, hating, or being afraid of. Getting angry results from splitting life in twain, and then claiming that half of one's own life is divine and the other half is demonic, and impossibly trying to make choice of the half. Zen reality can only be the holiness of life. It seeks for neither divine half nor demonic half but the wholeness; that is, the Divine. Seen from Zen's point of view, the state of division is hell. Getting angry, resulting from the wholeness, is equally heavenly. Not getting angry, resulting from the division, is equally hellish; that is, equally abstract, incomplete, equally inadequate to life's integral needs as its opposite. Hell is this condition of schizophrenia in which one is divorced from the other.

This fragmentation of life from the other can never be overcome by trying to make one-half of oneself supreme over the other half, or *vice versa.* When one tries to subject one-half of oneself to the other half, one is involved in anger, hatred, and fear, and is in denial of one's true self.

There is a Zen story to reveal the absence of worldly passions. There was a Japanese Zen teacher whose name was Hakuin. He was praised by his followers as one living the life of Zen. A beautiful Japanese girl lived near him. Her parent discovered she was pregnant. This made her parents angry. She did not confess who her lover was, but she finally named Hakuin after she had been harassed. In great anger the parents went to the teacher, and blamed him for that. "Is that so?" was all the teacher said. After the child was born, it was brought to Hakuin, who lost all his reputation. And yet the losing of his reputation did not trouble him a bit. Instead the teacher took very good care of the child. He visited his neighbors to obtain milk for the child. A year later, the girl-mother could not stand it any longer. She told her parents the truth, that the real father of the child was a young man who worked in the fishmarket. The parents of the girl at once went to Hakuin to seek his forgiveness and to get the child back again. The teacher was willing. All the teacher said was: "Is that so?"

There is another very interesting story, which is a parable on the effort to eradicate the half of one's own self. The devil undertakes to destroy a certain individual by a quite unusual device. This person is very sincere and is trying hard to get rid of his sins and his vices. The devil agrees to extract from him any vices, which he wants to have extracted. The man says, "I am very prone to anger and I wish I were not such an easily angered person." "Could not you do something about my anger?" "Oh, yes," says the devil. And he pulls out a kind of a thread from the man's body and says, "Now, there is your anger, what else?" "Well, I am very a jealous person." "Could you do something about my jealous nature?" "Oh, yes," and he pulls out the thread of jealousy and the man is no longer jealous. So the man goes through the whole catalogue of his vices and sins. And for every sin a thread comes out. At the end there is no human being left—just a mass of jelly, because somehow this so-called lower nature is the source of all vitality. It is as real and as necessary as his higher nature. And Zen aims to awaken the mind without making any choice between getting angry and not getting angry. When one is angry, one must BE ANGRY. When one is not angry, one must NOT try to get ANGRY. This is the meaning of being nonchalant either to injury or to treatment. Either getting angry half-heartedly or not getting angry half-heartedly is like a bolt of lightning from a white cloud. As St. Paul said, *Be angry, and yet do not sin. Do not let the sun go down on your anger.*

Case XLVIII. Endurance

Without endurance, Bodhisattvas' ten thousand deeds will not succeed.

Xishan's Commentary

Ways to cultivate are innumerable, but compassion and endurance are fundamental. However, enduring mind is like a puppet's dream, while insulting situation is like a turtle's hair.

Blowing Rock's Commentary

It is the Bodhisattva's vow not to enter nirvana until all living beings are saved. In order to fulfill the vow, a Bodhisattva must succeed in performing ten thousand deeds. These deeds consist of six categories: giving, keeping of the precepts, endurance, meditation, concentration, and wisdom. Out of these six, compassion and endurance are the most essential. Compassion is not merely sympathy but fundamentally relishing suffering. To relish suffering is to endure. Endurance means neither to get angry nor to blame. The life of Zen transcends the life of ego-centeredness. Realizing the truth that there is no real "ego" (anatta), there is no dualism of "I" and "You." Since there is no "I" who receives insults, where is the other who gives anyone any insult? The mind that tries to endure insults is a puppet's dream. The situation by which insults seem to be made is a turtle's hair. However, both a puppet's dream and a turtle's hair in reality do not exist.

Case XLIX. The Greatest Meditation

The greatest meditation is to maintain the original and true mind.

Xishan's Commentary

If anyone starts to think of doing meditation, it is not meditation but delusion. So it is said, "Do not delude yourself, do not delude yourself." The idle always look backward. Such a person gives up one's own self.

Blowing Rock's Commentary

Meditation is one of the six deeds which must be performed by a Bodhisattva to fulfill the vow. A Bodhisattva must always meditate oneself with genuine and pure mind. However, one must not entertain *the thought* of doing meditation and *the thing* to be meditated. Instead, one just meditates. It means non-duality between meditator and meditating deed. One should neither impose oneself on the meditation nor surrender oneself to the meditation. Otherwise, the meditator is either too big for the deed and appears like an ascetic, or the deed is too big for the meditator and one is dragged into it. A real meditator is neither a kind of sadist nor a kind of masochist. The real meditator is a person who is a way of being at one with the meditation.

Master Funyang (762–823) uniformly responded to all questions with the answer, "Do not deceive yourself, do not deceive yourself." The questions referred to are asking with the intellect. Asking with the intellect is deluding oneself. Many times, many people do not know the fact that they can deceive themselves in asking. Many times questioning is a way of avoiding the real answer, which is really known already. Every person is enlightened, but wishes one was not. Every person knows the basic principles of one's own religion, but one does not wish to know them. So one asks questions. That is why master Funyang kept repeating, "Do not deceive yourself."

If one is thinking about meditation, it is delusion. If one meditates with a pure mind that has cut off all thinking, then meditation is the reality. So is one's going to bathroom: all deeds are meditation. So Zen is maintaining the genuine mind, which is before thinking. One may have many intellectual questions about Zen. That is good. But if one is thinking that the questions may lead to enlightenment, then one misses Zen. Where the questions are asked, no answer is possible. Where the answer could be had, there is no question. Seen from this point of view, Anything that can be asked intellectually is deception.

Case L. Mantras

Karma made in one's present life can easily be controlled and thus corrected by one's own power. Karma accumulated in one's previous life cannot be easily erased without getting some help from divine power. Therefore, one recites mantras.

Xishan's Commentary

Madeng did indeed attain the fruition of enlightenment. Thus, it is difficult for anyone to avoid the obstacles of maras without reciting mantras.

Blowing Rock's Commentary

Unobstructed wisdom comes into evidence when deed, speech, and thought become true and pure. Mantras are like pray. One's mantra is no mere formality. One is not just going through certain standardized motions or mechanically repeating certain standardized spooky words, phrases, or texts. One's mantra should be the pioneering venture of the spirit or the absolutely genuine sound of a soul in need. The mere chirping of Sanskrit language is not a good thing. The genuine way of chanting mantra may be likened to a process of unlearning. Many people today are stuffed with external knowledge. The chanting of a mantra should help one to decrease external knowledge. As Lao Zi says in *the Dao De Jing*, *The student of knowledge aims at learning day by day; the student of Dao aims at losing day by day*. The vibrating chant of mantras shakes off whatever can be shaken, until nothing remains. Out of nothing, one can begin anew.

Madeng is matangi in Sanskrit. It refers to a female who belongs to one of the lowest castes in India. A male in the same caste is called Matanga. There was a matangi whose name was Prakriti. She enticed Ananda, one of the chief disciples of Buddha, into her room. At this time, Bodhisattva Wenshu started to chant mantras. With the assistance of mysterious power that resulted from the chant, both of them were saved from indulgence of sex. Later Prakriti shaved her head and made a new beginning. She joined the Buddhist community, and she became an enlightened person.

Case LI. Real Worship

Worship is nothing but reverence and submission. Namely, one reveres one's true nature, while one surrenders one's ignorance.

Xishan's Commentary

When body, speech, and will are all pure, that is Buddha's coming into the world.

Blowing Rock's Commentary

It is not necessary to be pure or impure in order to worship, unless it interferes. Anything that interferes with human life is impure or unclean. The greatest thing that hinders one from true worship is one's own ignorance about oneself. The idea of impurity rests upon the poor perception. When one says, "My hands are dirty," but in actuality it is not true. The dirt is outside the hands. Even if the dirt is injected into the blood, it is still separate from the blood itself. The blood is not dirty.

Can one have a dirty atom? So it is with one's true nature. That is the reason why Yunmen's "dried dung stick" was given to the question, "What is Buddha?" Even if someone pours dung on God, God cannot be contaminated with it. Likewise, one's true nature cannot be defiled by any deeds. One must worship one's true nature. This is perhaps what the New Testament indicates in cautioning humans; *God is spirit, and He must be worshiped in spirit and in truth.* Not to know this is the greatest ignorance. Ignorance is like the dirt in the wrong place. Dirt does not originate out of the true self but dwells on the true self. All that one has to do is to remove that dirt. That is the meaning of surrendering one's ignorance. Surrendering is a continuing process throughout the evolution of one's meditation.

Case LII. Invoking The Buddha

As for invoking the Buddha, doing it with a mouth is chirping; doing it with the mind is invoking the Buddha. Calling Buddha with one's mouth without thinking of him is of no use for the students of Dao.

Xishan's Commentary

"Emituofo," the dharma gate of these six characters, is the shortcut to free oneself from the cycle of transmigration. One's mind should not forget Buddha's world by thinking of it. One's mouth should not talk in delirium but call Buddha's name clearly and distinctly. It is the invocation of Buddha that the mind is in accord with the mouth.

Xishan's Further Commentary

The fifth patriarch said, "To maintain one's true mind is better than thinking of all the Buddhas everywhere." The sixth patriarch said, "One cannot escape the cycle of life-and-death by thinking of the external Buddhas; one can reach the other shore by keeping watch on one's true mind." He also said, "One becomes Buddha within one's nature, so do not seek him outside of one's body." Furthermore, he said, "The unenlightened tries to live by chanting Buddha's name, while the enlightened just purify one's own mind." Or, "All beings liberate themselves by awakening their minds; Buddha cannot liberate them."

The above-mentioned sages said nothing about different methods but instead about the direct pointing to the soul of a person. In principle, so it is. Nevertheless, in actuality, there are nirvana, Amitabha Buddha, and the forty-eight resolutions. So all the Buddhas of the triple world say unanimously that anyone who merely chants "Buddha" ten times will be born in a lotus bud and free from the cycle of birth-and-death by the power of the resolutions. All the Bodhisattvas of the ten directions desire to be born there. Moreover, through all ages, many people who had been in nirvana obviously left their biographical writings. Do not misunderstand.

The Sanskrit word "Emituo" means "infinite life," or "infinite light." It is the highest title of Buddha in the ten directions and the triple world. In his early life, he was called Dharmakara Bhikshu who made forty-eight resolutions before Lokesvaraja Buddha. He said,

> Attaining Buddhahood, I wish all the heavenly beings and people of all the ten directions even including tiny insects be born in my holy place just by their invoking of my name ten times. If this wish is not going to be met, I do not wish to attain Buddhahood.

A sage of old said,

> Just one note of chanting of Buddha's name will strike chill in devils' hearts. It will make one's name erased from the book of devil. And it will make the lotus emerge from the golden lake.

It is also said in *The Method of Penitence,*

> One's own power is slow; other's power is fast. It will take a long time to cross the sea by making a boat with a tree which one grows. It compares with one's own power. However, it will take a short time to cross the sea by borrowing a boat. It compares with the power of Buddha.

It is also said,

> The child cries loudly for help, when fire or waters threaten the child. Then, his/her parents hear and run to rescue the child. Likewise, One invokes Buddha loudly, when one is dying. Then, Buddha with his divine power will surely come to welcome oneself. The compassion of the all-holy one is deeper than that of parents, while the suffering of all beings in the cycle of birth-and-death is more severe than that of fire and waters.

Someone said,

> One's own mind is the pure land. What is the use of being born again in the pure land? One's nature is Amitabha. What is the use of trying to see Amitabha?

It seems to be right, but it is not so. The Buddha is neither greedy nor angry. Am I neither greedy nor angry? The Buddha can transform the hells into a lotus flower as easily as one turns over one's own palm. While I am afraid of falling into the hell due to my own karma, can I really transform the hells into the lotus world? The Buddha can see the endless universe as if it exists in front of his eyes. On the other hand, I cannot see even things right behind a wall. How can I see things in the world of the ten directions? Yes, everyone's nature is already Buddha, but one's actual deeds are still like an ordinary being. The difference between principle and actuality is that between heaven and earth. Master Guifeng (780–841) said, "Although one may be enlightened suddenly, one should cultivate oneself gradually until the end of one's life." Indeed, he spoke correctly.

Now let me talk to a person who says that my nature is Amitabha. If this were true, how could there be Sakyamuni, who was born miraculously? Or how could there be Amitabha, who was born in the natural way? Think of oneself, then one will see it of oneself. Does anyone really think of having perfect freedom in the middle of undergoing the great pain with the last breath? If not, one should be careful not to fall eternally into evil ways due to momentary pride. Even though Asvaghosha (about 100–160) and Nargajuna (150–250) were patriarchs, they obviously advised that one should sincerely desire rebirth in paradise. Then what kind of person am I who deny rebirth there? As Buddha himself said, "The western land is far from here, one must pass through ten million eight thousand nations." In such a case, he spoke about actuality for the ordinary people. At times, Buddha said, "The western land is not far, the mind (all beings) is the Buddha (Amitabha)." In such a case, he spoke about one's nature for the wise people.

In teaching, there are the existential and the essential. In words, there are the explicit and the implicit. Anyone, whose understanding is in accord with deeds, opens oneself universally into the way that is far away or close by. Therefore, even in the school of patriarchs, there was Huiyuan (334–416), who called on Amitabha Buddha, and Ruian, who relied upon his own self.

Blowing Rock's Commentary

The full six characters of "emituofo" are "Nanmuemituofo." One of many meanings of "Nammu" is "to return." "Emituo" means "infinite life" or "infinite light." Infinite life symbolizes compassion. Infinite light symbolizes wisdom. Both living compassion and bright wisdom symbolize the true original self. Seen from this point of view, the whole meaning of the chant means "to return to the true self which consists of wisdom and compassion."

The fifth patriarch of Zen is Hongren (605–675 A.D.). Among his disciples, Huineng and Shinshu were famous. Huineng represents the southern school of Zen, which is also called the sudden school, while Shinshu represents the northern school of Zen, which is also called the gradual school.

"Ten directions" are east, west, north, south, northeast, northwest, southeast, southwest, upward and downward. "The other shore" means nirvana, where one ceases to suffer. "This shore" is samsara, where one suffers life incessantly. Before Siddhartha was enlightened, he made the forty-eight resolutions to be characteristics of nirvanic place. Otherwise, he refused to be enlightened. Some of them are as follows: The first resolution is that there must be no suffering or pain. The third is that people in that place must have the same faces and the same bodies. The fifth, people in that place must be able to perform six mysterious tricks. The fifteenth, people in that place must have infinite life and infinite light. The eighteenth, people, wherever they live, chant "Buddha" just ten times, they will be born there. The thirty-third, whenever people receive the infinite light, both their minds and their bodies become beautiful. "Ten times" in chanting of Buddha's name means "fullness" or "completeness." Therefore, to chant Buddha's name ten times means to chant "Buddha" wholeheartedly. It means to chant "Buddha" with all one's mind, all one's body, and all one's thought. Triple world means past, present, and future.

Buddha is not something that can be grasped or adhered to. Buddha is living truth. Nothing that is real can be owned. One cannot possess a human being such as a friend, a husband, a wife, or a child. One cannot hold one's work. As soon as one is trying to hold on to anything, it becomes a corpse in one's hands. One can only grasp abstractions. The possessor is *external* to what one possesses. And then one converts that which one possesses into an object. Whenever one holds something, one does not let it live or grow. Buddha is Zen, that is, life itself. Life cannot be held. Nothing living can be owned.

One might think that a Zen master has knowledge of Zen. If he or she possesses knowledge of Zen, the master is not worth listening to. Knowledge that can be grasped can be put on tape. The tape will do as well as the master. If a Zen master possesses knowledge of Zen, the master is possessed by it. Master's relation to Zen is uncreative. The Zen master fixes Zen and it fixes him. However, the enlightened Zen master is in a living relationship to one's Zen. He or she does not possess it. Instead, one gives oneself to it creatively. One lives with it. One lets it live in oneself. One comes to life through it. It comes to life through oneself. In that case, one's Zen is not an abstract possession which can be put on tape. It is something inexhaustible, which can never be pinned down. So it is with friendship, marriage, or a hobby. So far as these things are realities, they are not possessions. They are callings, which offer one the opportunity to create and thereby to come alive.

To the degree that Zen is thought of as enshrining a truth as over against other opposing truth, the believer imagines oneself to possess that truth. One defines one's own being in relation to it. In that way, one limits one's own being and converts it into a kind of abstraction, that is, something defined in relation to an externality. And thus one lacks real basis in being truly oneself. One is ignorant of one's true identity. One is merely aware of oneself only through one's relationship to a Zen which one possesses. That Zen is not the Zen of one's own being. That Zen is really a label rather than a reality.

Zen Buddhism, which is thought of as enshrining the essence of Buddhism, is a pose or a posturing. To feel oneself only in terms of one's own position is to be anchored in abstractions. Real identity is of the spirit, and so far as one is afraid to encounter the spirit, one seeks a false identity through *this or that* Zen labels. Since the identity is not real, one is always in peril of being exposed. So there is fearfulness. A fanaticism based on fear lurks in the background of every position. The living Zen is never defensive. It never feels opposed or threatened. A truly enlightened Zen person has nothing to defend. One is not grasping onto anything, which might be torn out of one's hands. The true Zen person has only one's life to live and one's own reality to communicate.

One sometimes sees people achieve a certain degree of strength and integrity through holding to a Zen position. Ultimately it is not *real* strength or integrity. All of us must have witnessed something like the incident which I am going to describe. It brings out vividly the difference between a facade of virtue and natural virtue. One of my teachers was present at an interreligious conference at which there were representative of all the world's major faiths. Among the participants, he observed one lady who had been a missionary to India and who had a very radiant face, which had been shaped by a life of service. He was so struck by her appearance that he mentioned it to several people. He was one of the speakers at that conference. He had been asked to speak about Zen Buddhism. Although he did not speak with any idea of converting anybody, what he said somehow threatened this woman. During the question period, her face was absolutely transformed. She snarled at him. He saw that after all she had fangs. Something that he said or the way in which he said it, had threatened her security and her identity. At once, her peace and serenity disappeared. In other words, they were not fully real to begin with. She had them only so long as she was not threatened. So there is the difference between appearance and reality. Reality can never be threatened. It never feels insecure. Whenever one comes to real self-identity on the basis of the spirit, one is adequate to all circumstances.

Though the story concerned a Christian missionary to India, there is no need to mention that the same principle applies to everyone who possesses religion. Zen as reality does not occupy a position. If one wants one's Zen to be more than a pose, one has to get *beyond* the Zen position. And getting beyond it does not mean discarding it. It is because one would merely be adopting another position. Monism, monotheism, solipsism, pluralism, agnosticism, mysticism, or atheism is just as much a position and a pose as Zen Buddhism. Getting *beyond* the position means getting *into* it so deeply that one comes to the spiritual core of it, which is no mere label. Then it cannot be threatened. One will have no need to show one's fangs. This is perhaps what the New Testament indicates in cautioning Christians that *the letter kills, but the spirit gives life*. Any position must be "spiritualized." Only then, it does become truly one's own. And it becomes no more an external imposition. When it is spiritualized, one no longer even knows what it is, because it is not a *what*, that is, an abstraction or a definable content. It is nothing one attaches or feels called upon to defend. Only then one experiences the perfect love which casts all fear and all fanaticism.

It is human tendency that one is afraid to live out of one's own naked reality. However, all reality is naked. It was only after Adam and Eve fell that they became ashamed of their nakedness. They covered it over. Real Zen life is the life of authenticity, which is the fruit of the spirit. Authentic life is to surrender to the spirit. This surrendering to the spirit is called "Emituofo." It has no citizenship paper, no identifying tags, no recipes, or no descriptions. It is life creating itself. It is ringing true. It is life before it is crystallized into forms and Zen.

Zen position is an idol in relation to the truth of the spirit. It as a pose is an inadequate substitute for the living truth. Anyone who puts one's faith in a system is fearful of encountering Being. From this point of view, let it be said that organized or institutionalized religion has most often been the enemy of spiritual life. Spiritual freedom derives from the spirit itself. It will not be one's own if one shuns living truth and settles for abstract truth.

Case LIII. Hearing *The Sutras*

One's hearing of *the Sutras* causes words to pass through one's own ears, and one is attended by the blessing of joy. Foamy body will be exhausted, but the real conduct does not end.

Xishan's Commentary

This is to explain a wise study. It is likened to eating a diamond, which is better than possessing seven jewels. Master Yongming (904–975) said, "Even though one listens without any faith, the seed of Buddha has been planted in oneself: even though one studies without any success, one will still surpass both the human and the heavenly blessings."

Blowing Rock's Commentary

The hearing of *the Sutras* can help one find a center which restores oneself to one's integrity, if such a hearing is authentic; that is, rooted in a full dimension of oneself. To really let the words of *the Sutras* pass through ears is to give oneself to the absolute relationship with life itself. In other words, genuine hearing comes into being, when it is not controlled by the intellect. The hearing of *the Sutras* is neither just a matter of collecting information nor of having a certain set of ideas. Nor is the hearing of *the Sutras* controlled by just a funny feeling, because feeling is something that is not at one's beck and call. The hearing, which brings the blessing of joy, must be grounded on one's wholeness. Every set of ideas and funny feelings are fragments of one's self. Therefore, ideas or feelings cannot be an absolute ground of hearing. Real hearing is spiritual.

In fact, it occurs to me that it would be possible to restate master Yongming's words so as to emphasize the spirit of the case even more pointedly. Spiritual hearing is not a matter of faith in Buddha or his words, because faith is the suppression of doubt. The reason that one has faith is because one doubts. If one did not have any doubt, one would not have any faith. The faith is the covering up of the doubt or the pushing of the doubt to the rear of one's mind. The doubt is still there. The struggle between doubt and faith is still there. Belief is taking a stand on some ideas that one has formed. And one forces to suppress any doubts that one may have about the ideas. There is no such thing as a wholehearted belief in Buddha or *the Sutras*. Only irreligious people who have indocile ears believe in *the Sutras*. A religious person is united to the spirit of the words of *the Sutras*. In my new version of the statement made by master Yongming, it is because of listening without any faith in Buddha or his words that one is accompanied with Buddha. It is because of studying without any success that one has to begin anew.

Likewise, wise studies, unlike secular studies, are not based on research. Wise studies are not researching but spiritual searching. In spiritual seeking, that which is sought after does not exist apart from the real conduct of searching for it. The two are ultimately one. Hearing *about the Sutras* is not the same thing as living *the Sutras,* just as possessing of seven jewels is not the same thing as the eating of a diamond. When one possesses *the Sutras'* words and repeats them to others, somehow the words do not sound as they did on the lips of the original Buddha. The reason is that one possesses the words and that one's own being is not united with the words.

Case LIV. Reading *The Sutras*

If one reads *the Sutras* without inquiring within, even the reading of the eighty thousand volumes of *the Tripitaka* will be of no use.

Xishan's Commentary

This is to explain a foolish study. It is likened to the chirping of birds on a spring day or the crying of insects on an autumn night. Master Zongmi said, "Reading *the Sutras* with knowledge of words cannot awaken one. Selecting phrases with interpretation of their meanings merely increase greed, anger and perverted opinions."

Blowing Rock's Commentary

One of the greatest hindrances to the religious life is a misconception concerning the kind of truth which the religious life involves. So many people look upon Zen Buddhism as a package of general or objective truths. They hope to make their own lives truthful by participating in a kind of joint ownership of the package of truth. In this way, no genuine spiritual liberation can ever be achieved, because no one can achieve a valid self-identity by adhering to something which is other than one's own self.

One of the limitations inherent in *the Sutras* is that they tend to point to a Buddha who is external to life. Life must be concretely lived by the individual. There is one's own self, and there is life to be lived. What more is needed? There are many novelists, theologians, psychologists, psychiatrists, philosophers, and teachers of religions. Their study of *the Sutras*, and their study of the meaning of sanity or the way to a good life, is very detailed and profound, and yet they themselves, despite all the research, have not been able to overcome their alienation from life. They do not themselves embody the truth which they expound so well.

In Zen, any study without inquiring within is a foolish one. The spiritual life, that is, the living truth, must somehow express one's own individuality. It cannot do so, unless one has a hand in shaping it. One can never with perfect sincerity bow to a Buddha who is other than oneself. Religions of West Asia have never fully faced up to the full implications of this fact. A true answer to life's problem must be forged in the context of one's life. *The truth* of one's life must be the truth of one's own life. Since all the founders of world religions did imitate no one, one must not imitate them either. Zen is not something that one can imitate. Zen does not encourage one to imitate. Zen wants one to be oneself, that is, to be creative.

However, each individual does absorb something of the spirit of *the Sutras*. *The Sutras* function to purify one's individual self, which has been amalgamated with greed, anger, and opinion. Religion, which ignores one's individual existence, is abstract. If religion ignores *the scandal of one's individuality*, it tends to emphasize on terms which are objective, general, numerical, predictive, and controllable. Since life is inescapably concrete and individual, *the Sutras,* which are couched in those terms, bypass life.

Case LV. Foolish Study

If one tries to win over others by playing with words in order to boast of studying even before one's study reaches for enlightenment, it is likened to decorating a bathroom with colors.

Xishan's Commentary

This is especially to explain about foolish study in the end of the world. Studying is originally for cultivating one's own nature. What nonsense if it is only to show off!

Blowing Rock's Commentary

"The end of the world" means degenerate age when there is decline in physical, mental, or spiritual qualities. A student of Dao should inquire within. Otherwise, one tends to externally brag about it. If one worries about one's own fame, one is not a student of Dao but a half-hearted showman. A half-hearted showman's life depends upon a trifling or ephemeral fame. It is likened to painting one's bathroom. The *raison d'etre* of bathroom is not to beautify it but to pass water or to ease oneself. Decorating of a toilet can be made externally inasmuch as physical discomforts can be alleviated from without. If one is hungry, food can be provided. If one is in pain, aspirin can get rid of it. However, this is not how Zen life works. Enlightenment cannot be given from the outside. It must be reached by oneself. It follows that it is impossible to do Zen for another. No one cultivates or purifies another as no one can go to the bathroom for others. One can argue with others about an idea of whether the bathroom is in need of decoration or not. However, one should not argue with a person who is in dire need of going to the bathroom. Huineng said:

> This truth is to be lived, it is not to be merely pronounced with the mouth. There is really nothing to argue about in this teaching; Any arguing is sure to go against the intent of it. Teachings given up to controversy and argumentation lead of themselves to birth and death.

Case LVI. Studying Outer Writings

One, who leaves behind one's own home and studies outer writings, is likened to cutting mud with a knife. The mud is of no use, while the knife ruins itself.

Xishan's Commentary

Having played outdoor games, a wealthy person's children return to their house which is on fire.

Blowing Rock's Commentary

One who leaves behind one's own house is a Buddhist monk. The deeper meaning of getting out of one's own home is to be liberated from one's desire, one's aversion, and one's own ignorance. In other words, it means spiritual freedom from all sorts of clinging.

Outer writings refer to non-scriptural writings. Many monks, who forget and neglect their own station in life, pay too much attention to the external affairs. Without reading of the scriptural writings, such monks try to buy magazines, weekly or monthly, from shopkeepers, and to comment on the worldly affairs with their own perverted opinions. Such monks neglect to inquire within to listen to the tiny small voice from their inner self, because of their paying too much attention to worldly noise. It is likened to cutting mud with a knife.

The quote "A wealthy person's children return to their houses which is on fire," comes from one of the Buddhist *Sutras*: A rich person came home from his business trip. He saw his house on fire. However, his children were absorbed in playing inside of their house. He yelled out, warning them to come out of the house. They did not pay any attention to their father's warning. Finally he used two toy vehicles to lure them out of the house. He put the children on the big toy vehicle and carried them to a safer place. The little toy vehicle symbolizes the Hinayana Buddhism, while the great toy vehicle symbolizes Mahayana Buddhism. Both vehicles tend to carry people from this world (samsara) to other world (nirvana). If a monk, who left behind his home, allows himself to be influenced by the worldly things, he is likened to children who return to their own home on fire.

Case LVII. Not A Trivial Thing

It is not a trivial thing that one leaves home to become a monk. It is not for an idle living, warm clothing, hot meals, or fortune and fame. It is for liberating from life and death, cutting off worldly passions, maintaining Buddha's wisdom, and getting out of the triple world to save living beings.

Xishan's Commentary

What a man he is! He pierces heaven.

Blowing Rock's Commentary

There is no need to argue here that one among human distinctive marks is human inability to live by bread, wealth, or fame alone and to ignore questions about the meaning of one's life and one's own final destiny. This salient mark is so obvious to religious people whose natures are built in spiritual tropism. No matter how much one may possess the ordinary goods of life, one will continue to feel basic inquietude so long as one has not come to terms with the ultimate mysteries. Human inescapable need is to have some sense of life's final meaning and to come into relationship with that meaning.

One, who wishes to be a monk, must initially realize such an intrinsic value of quest for the meaning of life. Many monks today have forgotten how to ask such an intrinsic quest. And they live in the triple world which consists of three poisons: desire, aversion, and ignorance. In the world of desire, there are three basic elements: lust, greed, and grasping. If one resides in this world, one's mind will be contaminated by these three elements. In the world of aversion, there are three basic elements: anger, hatred, and fear. One who lives in this world may be free of desire, and yet one is subject to aversion. In the world of ignorance, there may be neither desire nor aversion. However, there yet remains the impenetrable ego consciousness. Therefore, anyone who lives in this triple world is not totally free from the watertight egoism. Zen helps one to be free from the three poisons.

Furthermore, one may ask about ultimate matters of life and death externally, that is, from an intellectual position. The only reply is twofold: one is that from where the question is asked, no answer is possible. The other is that from where the answer could be had, there is no question. To be a monk means to force one's own self to go on to the very end of one's own existential quest. The closer one gets to the spiritual core of the quest, the more one lives the reality of life and death.

Case LVIII. Three Great Defects

Buddha said, "The flame of impermanence burns all the world." He said again, "Sufferings of all living beings catch fire from all sides." He also said, "The thieves of all worldly passions always peep at people to kill." The students of Dao must awaken themselves, as if they extinguish the fire on their heads.

Xishan's Commentary

The body is to be born, to grow old, to be diseased, and to die. The world is to arise, to continue, to break down, and to vanish. The mind is to appear, to linger, to differentiate, and to disappear. All these mean that impermanence and sufferings catch fire from all sides. O, truth seekers! Do not pass time idly!

Blowing Rock's Commentary

The Buddha provided his basic reasons why one should extinguish the flame of life. He taught that all living beings are vexed by three great defects: impermanence (anicca), the unreality of ego (anatta), and suffering (dukkha). These three are interchangeably related to each other. The one follows the other two. The body, the world, and the mind are subject to the endless change (anicca). The ceaseless becoming provides no place for a solid substance (anatta), which in turn fills lives with suffering (dukkha). Figuratively speaking, the unenlightened life is likened to a crazy person who runs wild (anicca). It is also likened to that person who gets drunk (anatta). Furthermore, it is like that same person who is stung by a wasp (dukkha).

So the Buddha felt that it is ignorance to be attached with worldly passions (tanha) to the living beings. He said that worldly passions should be ended to extinguish the flames of impermanence and suffering. He succinctly expressed the cause of the flames and the way to extinguish them in the Four Noble Truths. The Four Noble Truths are his first sermon made to the five ascetics in the Deer Park at Benares. They are as follows:

> This, O monks, is the first Noble truth of suffering. Birth is suffering; old age is suffering; disease is suffering; death is suffering. Presence of things one hates is suffering; absence of things one likes is suffering. The fivefold clinging to existence is suffering.

> This, O monks, is the second Noble Truth of the cause of suffering. Passion that leads to rebirth, accompanied by pleasure and lust, finding its delight here and there. This passion is threefold: passion for pleasure, passion for existence, and passion for prosperity.
> This, O monks, is the third Noble Truth of the end of suffering; the complete end of this passion.
> This, O monks, is the Fourth Noble Truth of the Eightfold Path which leads to the end of suffering: right belief, right aspiration, right speech, right conduct, right livelihood, right effort, right mindfulness, and right meditation.

In a nutshell, Eightfold Path consists of right wisdom, right cultivation, and right meditation. It functions to remove all mixture of gases and particles of worldly carbon monoxide, which rises when three poisons burn without a sufficient supply of enlightenment. With the final extinction of the flames of three poisons, the mind begins to see things as they really are.

Case LIX. Desiring The Worldly

To desire transient worldly fame is to afflict one's own body. To struggle for worldly profit is to add kindling for the karmic flames.

Xishan's Commentary

A poem said about desiring transient worldly fame:

The geese flew away into the sky,
Leaving their footprints on the sand.
People passed away into the other world,
Leaving their names with the family.

Another poem said about struggling for worldly profit:

After honey is collected from a hundred flowers,
Know not who tastes its bitterness?

Afflicting one's own body is of no use, as if one tries to create a work of art by carving ice. Adding kindling for the karmic flame means that all things filled with colors and perfumes in fact are fuels added to the flames.

Blowing Rock's Commentary

The Bible says, *Do not love the world or anything in the world. The cravings of the world and its desires pass away, but the man who does the will of God lives forever.* To desire the worldly fame is ephemeral, as if the wild geese leave their footprints on the sand. To strive for the mundane profit is precarious, as if one's own food can be poisonous to others. In other words, *The New Testament* forbids humans to love the world, because it is impermanent. The case mentioned above forbids humans to desire or struggle for the worldly fame and profit, because it will be a cause of suffering. However, one will be making a fatal mistake if one does not caution oneself about the meaning of words such as "love," "desire," or "struggle." *The Bible* says that one should not give oneself with passion to all those things, which the world counts so dear: sexual pleasure, money, position, fame, wealth, and power.

However, one can take these words with deeper meaning. One may love the world, the things of the world, all of them without exception, but one should not love them for the pleasure they give or hate them for the suffering they bring oneself. In a nutshell, one can love them without attachment. To desire the worldly fame or to struggle for the worldly profit means this attached love. It is the love found in the statement that *the love of money is the root of all evil.* The attached desire or struggle means selfish love as opposed to pure love. The selfish love means accumulative, willful, and deliberate possession with reference to past, present, or future.

Furthermore, one should be able to make clear distinction between false detachment and pure detachment. A false detachment comes from deep selfishness, which avoids all genuine love, because love may lead to sacrifice or suffering. It is like a kind of drone who tries to get all the honey of life with none of its poison or the rose without the thorns. A pure detachment is love without attachment. An example of a pure detachment is giving not for pleasure of giving but simple, thoughtless, instinctive giving. In this love, one is not aware that one gives, nor of what one gives, not to whom one gives, still less of whether it is appreciated by the recipient or not. In a pure detachment, there is a trinity, a single action with all these parts undifferentiated in its activity.

Case LX. A Ragged Monk

A ragged monk who follows fame and fortune is worse than a country-bred person who wears grass clothing.

Xishan's Commentary

Spitting at a king's palace to go into the snowy mountain is an unchangeable rule, even though the Buddha would be born a thousand times. In the end of the world, the multitude of sheep nature, who wears a tiger's skin on, tries to flatter to win favor without a sense of honor and to be blown about by the power struggle. Ah! What a pity! Anyone whose mind is stained with worldly profit does flatter at the gate of the powerful and is pestered by worldly affairs. The crowd laughs at that monk. The reason why such a monk is likened to the sheep nature is because such a monk has many plausible activities.

Blowing Rock's Commentary

This case is talking about either the ignorant or the hypocritical monks. The majority of monks today do not really try very hard to make their life consistent with their vows whatever they may be. A monk will tell the other that these are the teachings of Hinayana Buddhism. Another monk will tell that those are the vows of Mahayana Buddhism. The principles may differ to some extent that there are many schools of Buddhism. However, monks in general do not differ very much, because they have not really made their principal vows their *own*. One has not made oneself over in accordance with the teachings of one's respective school of Buddhism. For the majority of monks, there is an unawareness of the impossibility of developing an unqualified allegiance to the teachings of Buddhism. Otherwise, there is a kind of hypocritical pretense that their vows have been fulfilled. Such a hypocritical pretense means "sheep nature who wears a tiger's skin." In neither case, does one get really religious effort.

Case LXI. Nicknames Given To Monks

The Buddha lamented and said, "How badly thieves, who clothe themselves like me and sell me, make many kinds of wicked karma!"

Xishan's Commentary

This is the reason why many monks in the end of the world have many nicknames, such as "bat monk," "dumb goat monk," "tonsured hermit," "hellish trash," or "thief in a robe." To sell the Tathagata means to deny the law of causation, to deny sin and blessing, to make many kinds of karma with one's body and one's mouth like boiling water, and to give rise to love and hate incessantly. What a pity! Anyone who pretends neither to be a monk nor to be a layperson is called a "bat monk." Though one has a tongue, one who does not preach the Dharma is called a "dumb goat monk." One who has a monk's appearance with a layperson's mind is called a "tonsured hermit." One who has sinned heavily and thus is unable to move around is called "hellish trash." One who puts the Buddha on sale for a living is called a "thief in a robe." Because all such thieves wear the monk's robe, they receive many such nicknames.

Blowing Rock's Commentary

One of the many meanings of the word "monk" is a person who begs for one's bread. Such a begging person in the early history of Buddhism has a fivefold vow:

1. Do not possess private wealth.
2. Break off worldly passion and delusion.
3. Get out of the house of worldly passion, which is fired by desire, aversion, and ignorance.
4. Keep the Buddha's precepts.
5. Do not deviate from the right path.

Any monk who does not keep the vow is a hypocrite. A hypocrite is a person who pretends to be what one is not. A hypocritical monk does not like to endure willingly the pangs of creative seeking for Buddha nature. If a monk seeks Buddha nature, one will have to endure willingly the pains of keeping the vow. In other words, an authentic monk is one who will have to create one's own way to attain Buddhahood in the very keeping of the vow. As one gives oneself to the search, one does not withhold oneself. One does give up looking elsewhere. And thus one does not look to others for an external answer that will relieve one of the privilege and the burden of creating. In a nutshell, hypocritical monks do make an outward show of Buddhism without its real spirit. They are pharisaical.

What God requires of each individual is that one should knock oneself out one's whole life long to find out what is required of oneself. Until one does that, one is not really being honest to Buddha. Otherwise, one is trying to get by with something less than what is really required. In other words, one is trying to come by reality at bargain basement prices. Nevertheless, Buddha, that is, enlightenment, is never on sale. And its price is never marked down. One is required to sell all that one has, in order to be able to pay for it.

Case LXII. Receiving Almsgiving

O, Children of Buddha! One bowl of rice and one piece of clothing are the blood of farmers and the toil of woman weavers. How can one consume them without keen eyesight of Dao?

Xishan's Commentary

The Record of the Transmission of the Lamp said, "An ancient student of Dao became a mushroom after his death to repay his almsgiver's grace, because he did not have keen eyesight of Dao."

Blowing Rock's Commentary

All living beings are children of Buddha, because they possess the original Buddha nature within themselves. All humans inherit One Thing with its fivefold property. First, their trust in Buddha becomes an egg. Second, wisdom becomes its mother. Third, meditation becomes its womb. Fourth, compassion becomes its nurse. Fifth, Buddha becomes its father.

The Record of the Transmission of the Lamp is also called *The Zhuandenglu* in Chinese. It was composed by Yongan Daoyuan, who was one of the disciples of Tiantai Deshao. Deshao was one of the masters of Fayan School. It was revised by Yangyi. It covers the teachings and lives of many enlightened persons such as the seven Buddhas, Fayan Wenyi, and many masters of five Zen schools. During Sung Dynasty in China, this book was included in *the Tripitakas* in 1004 A. D.

One with keen eyesight of Dao sees that everybody is Buddha. The vision enables one to see nonduality between self and other: A child of Buddha embodies the toil of people with a grain of rice and a piece of clothing. And thus, one embraces both self and other. In other words, one loves other as oneself. One who does not see this fact of truth is unable to love oneself and other as well. When one's relationship to other is one of loving union, the problem of rebirth does not arise. On the contrary, when there is a separation between self and other, it is an indication that one does wrongly identify oneself with only a half aspect of the true self. Until one solves the identity crisis, one will be subject to the vicious cycle of rebirth.

Case LXIII. What One Needs Is Not What One Wants

Therefore, it is said, "What is it that wears fur and horns? It is what one will be if one consumes almsgivers' food without paying anything." It is a pity that some people eat even though they are not hungry and that they put on clothes even though they are not cold. They do not even suspect that their immediate pleasure will be the future suffering.

Xishan's Commentary

The Zhilun says, "Because of the five grains of millet, a student of Dao became a cow to toil hard in life and left hide and meat in death." What is owed has to be repaid.

Blowing Rock's Commentary

The Zhilun is also called *The Mahaprajnaparamita Sastra*. There is nothing free in the world. Otherwise, the cosmos will become chaos. One of the greatest vices in the current Buddhist institutions is consuming food without paying anything in return. Without doing what is required of oneself as a monk, one eats three meals a day. That is why there are many idlers. There are many people who are really hungry, and yet monks worry if the meals are offered on the scheduled time. *One day of no work is one day of no eating*. This has to be the conscience of monastery and the basic rule of everyday life as well.

Case LXIV. A Bodhisattva's Resolution

Therefore, it is said that one should prefer wearing hot iron to wearing the clothes given by the faithful, and that one should prefer drinking molten iron to eating the food given by the faithful, and that one should prefer jumping into a boiling cauldron to staying in the house built by the faithful.

Xishan's Commentary

The Fanwangjing says, "Make up one's mind not to receive any food or offering from the faithful when one has broken the precepts." "If a Bodhisattva does not make such a resolution, one commits a sin of impurity."

Blowing Rock's Commentary

The Fanwangjing is also known as *The Brahmajala Sutra.* If one lives the Zen life, every situation presents oneself with an invitation to enter into reality. If one's aim is merely to get around the situation, one will deal with it externally. The alms given by the faithful are invitations to enter into a truthful relationship with the spirit of the situation. Therefore, one has to give oneself totally to it. Otherwise, the alms become a third thing existing between oneself and the Zen life. So every gift is an invitation to enter into the spirit of every situation. One should not try to circumvent the invitation by applying external etiquette. This will not forge a true relationship with the faithful. In this context, one does well to be mindful to the ever-present possibility of gaining the whole world through hypocritical etiquette and losing one's soul.

If one is seeking a real encounter, then one must confront the spiritual invitation represented by the gift. No ordinary resourcefulness will affect the entry into reality except complete giving of oneself. In Zen, this complete giving of oneself is called "The Great Death." It is the great death to wear hot iron, to drink molten iron, and to jump into a boiling cauldron. One might also call it the great rebirth. It is a death to the old Adam or old ego, which stood outside of life, tried to manipulate life, and desired to receive the gifts from the faithful. Without the great death, there is no great awakening. If one wants to be Buddha, one has to die to one's externality.

As one continues to seek a real relationship with the faithful, one has to become progressively more free from ulterior motives. It is when one is totally devoid of gimmicks that one becomes poor in spirit or pure in heart. When one is utterly purified in spirit, then the kingdom of heaven is one's own.

Case LXV. Proper Way To Receive Alms

Therefore, it is said that a person of Dao should take food as if one were taking poison, and that one should receive alms as if one were taking an arrow. One should fear generous hospitality and honeyed words.

Xishan's Commentary

One needs to eat food as if one were eating poison, because one is afraid of losing the eye of Dao. One needs to receive alms as if one were receiving an arrow, because one is afraid of losing the fruit of Dao.

Blowing Rock's Commentary

A real person must realize the fact that alms should not be stored in a grain elevator. Food should be eaten enough to continue one's spiritual training. Money should not be saved in a bank, but it should be used to be current among the people.

Food and alms are not given free of charge. One must know that there are no free food nor free gifts. When one accounts one's whole life, one is either in the red or in the black. If one finds oneself being in the red, it is not because of chance but because of one's neglect to repay the debt of gratitude. One's endless cycle of life-and-death will never be ended until the debt is repaid. The way for the spiritual person to repay the debt is to attain enlightenment or reality. Otherwise, one will be poisoned by the arrow of rebirth and subject to the endless cycle of suffering.

Reality cannot be seen if one insists on a life of one's own externally. If one wants to attain true enlightenment, one has to die to one's externality. To die to one's externality is to see food and alms as Buddha sees them. That is the function of the eye of Dao. In other words, one has not to treat them as external objects to be possessed. One has to bear the fruits by way of appropriate eating of food or appropriate distribution of alms. It is not appropriate to glut oneself with the gifts. The non-duality of taking and giving is the fruit of Dao. In other words, to receive alms as Buddha did is to bear the fruit of Dao. However, one must remember that the fruit and the eye are one. The fruits are not the rewards which come as a result of seeing Dao. The fruits are the different aspects of seeing the way.

Case LXVI. A Whetstone

Therefore, it is said, "A student of Dao is likened to a whetstone. Mr. Zhang and Mr. Li come and sharpen their knives on the whetstone. They come and go away. Their knives are sharpened, but the whetstone gradually wears out. However, some people worry whether others come and sharpen their knives on their own whetstone. What a pity!"

Xishan's Commentary

Such students of Dao worry about having a full stomach and keeping themselves warm for their entire life.

Blowing Rock's Commentary

Jesus said:

> Therefore I tell you, do not worry about your life, what you will eat or drink; or about your body, what you will wear. Is not life more important than food, and the body more important than clothes? Look at the birds of the air; they do not sow or reap or store away in barns, and yet your heavenly Father feeds them. Are you not much more valuable than they? Who of you by worrying can add a single hour to his life?
>
> And why do you worry about clothes? See how the lilies of the field grow. They do not labor or spin. Yet I tell you that not even Solomon in all his splendor was dressed like one of these. If that is how God clothes the grass of the field, which is here today and tomorrow is thrown into the fire, will he not much more clothe you, O you of little faith? So do not worry, saying, 'What shall we eat?' or 'What shall we drink?' or, 'What shall we wear?' For the pagans run after all these things, and your heavenly Father knows that you need them. But seek first his kingdom, and his righteousness, and all these things will be given to you as well. Therefore do not worry about tomorrow, for tomorrow will worry about itself. Each day has enough trouble of its own.

Case LXVII. Losing One's Body

Therefore, as the old saying goes, "The suffering of the three evil ways is not real: To lose a human body after having worn the robe is real suffering."

Xishan's Commentary

An ancient sage said, "If one does not enlighten one's mind in one's present life, it will be difficult for one to digest even a drop of water." This is to lose a human body after having worn the stole. Oh, students of Buddha, Work hard as hell!

Blowing Rock's Commentary

In order to be enlightened, one has to be born as a human. To be born as humans is the best opportunity not to be wasted. Furthermore, to become a monk is the greatest opportunity to make the implicit enlightenment explicit. The real problem is not whether one will go to heaven but how to be a really human being. Otherwise, one will be living in three evil ways: hell, hungry ghosts, and animals. In other words, the three evil ways are likened to the situation where one lives a greedy life like hungry dogs fighting for a bone. One who wears the Buddhist robe should not worry about one's material needs. Buddhist temple is not an employment center but a center for humanhood. Hell is nothing but the condition of split between enlightenment and worldly passions, in which one has more than one face. In hell, one tries to make one fragment of life (worldly comforts) supreme over another fragment of life (enlightenment) or *vice versa*.

Buddhism is made for the wholeness of human being, which is nothing but the enlightenment. In other words, human being is not made for any form of religion. Furthermore, Buddha is for the enlightenment of human being; Human being is not made for Buddha. The only ultimate goal of human life is to live and express the enlightened life fully. Anything that furthers the enlightened life is legitimate, while everything that impoverishes the life of enlightenment must be rejected. *The Bible* says:

> Continue to work out your salvation with fear and trembling, for it is God who works in you to will and to act according to his good purpose.

Case LXVIII. How Funny It Is To Have A Body!

How funny it is to have a body! Dirt flows continually from nine holes. Hundreds and thousands of blotches are enveloped in a piece of thin hide. Furthermore, this leather bag is filled with dung. The lump of blood and pus stinks and is filthy. So it is neither desirable nor valuable. Though one's body is nurtured for a hundred years, it betrays in a single breath.

Xishan's Commentary

The above-mentioned karma all comes from having a body. One should scold oneself with a loud voice and awaken oneself. This body is the source of every passionate longing. If one realizes the nothingness of the body, the passions will vanish of themselves. Innumerable errors, worries, and anxieties arise from one's attachment to the body. Therefore, this point is specially mentioned in order for the students of Dao to open their eyes.

Xishan's Further Commentary

As this body, composed of the great four elements, has no master, it is regarded as fourfold enemy. As the great four are ungrateful, the body is regarded as the feeder of four snakes. I am angry with people, or look down on them, because I do not understand the nothingness of my body. They are angry with me, or look down on me, because they do not understand the untruth of their own bodies. It is likened to two ghosts who are fighting against each other over one corpse. The corpse is called "a bundle of froth," "a roll of dreams," "a bag of suffering," or "a heap of sludge." It is quickly subject to decay and is filthy to one's disgust. Tears, nasal mucus, and saliva constantly flow from the upper seven holes. Urine and dung are constantly discharged from the lower two holes. Therefore, one must purify one's body night and day in order to be with people. It is said that good spirits turn against those who are not clean.

It is said in *The Yinguojing (The Sutra of the Causes and Actions)*: "Those who pick up *the Sutras* with unclean hands or spit before the Buddha will be born as maggots next life." It is said in *The Wenshujing (The Manjusri Sutra)*: "When one relieves nature, like a tree or a rock, no one should speak, make a noise, scribble on the wall, or spit indiscriminately." It also said: "Without washing oneself clean after coming out of the lavatory, one should neither sit on the meditation room nor enter the sanctuary."

Blowing Rock's Commentary

The greatest and most tragic mistake is to think that the non-attachment to the body is something that one can achieve by asceticism. Asceticism is to mortify oneself to be in conformity with Buddha's law. Asceticism at times has afflicted Buddhism and other religions of the world. Many monks have tried to achieve the non-attachment to the body by willfully flagellating one's body, fasting, enduring pain, or sleeplessness. The real kind of non-attachment means the birth of the unconditional union with the body. The absolute reconciliation with the body is that which Zen requires. It is not something that can be achieved by any kind of ascetic exercise. Asceticism is always a part of oneself whipping the other part. This is not the spirit of Buddhism, or that of Zen Buddhism in particular. That is a kind of masochism.

In all religions of the world to some degree, people have thought that the slaying of the ego is the way of detachment from the body. However, there is only one way to get the spirit of detachment. And that is to overcome the false dualism of oneself from the body. That is to say, one has to overcome the standing outside of body. One has to be restored to the state of living oneness with body. The task of Zen is to achieve this restoration. One enters into the body to such an extent that there is no "I" and "no-body," that is, the nothingness of the body. The nothingness of the body is enlightenment, which is the overcoming of the gap between the body and the mind. That can never be resulting from any kind of self-torture. Buddhism has been guilty of the most horrible excess in this regard.

Case LXIX. Repentance

When one sins, repent. When one makes a mistake, be ashamed of it. This is the spirit of a great man. If one corrects one's mistake and begins anew, the karmic sin will vanish as one's mind does.

Xishan's Commentary

Repentance means both to be sorry for previous mistakes and to vow not to commit them again. "Being ashamed of" means both to scold oneself inwardly and express it outwardly. Since the mind is originally empty and calm, there is no place for sins to dwell.

Blowing Rock's Commentary

Real repentance is to feel sorry enough to quit. Real shame is to make the implicit explicit. In real repentance, there is no gap between feeling and action. In real shame, there is no gap between the implicit and the explicit. The spirit of a great personality is the transparency of personality, namely, absolutely direct, unreserved, uncalculating, uncontrived, unhesitating and always to the point. The person of this quality expects the same kind of response from others and helps others to inspire it. When a student of Dao is not able to match the spirit of the great person, one feels ashamed of one's own hollowness and inauthenticity.

The wobbling of the mind causes all sins to arise. When the mind is calm, all mistakes will vanish of themselves. The mind that is able to be ashamed of its wobbling is the hallmark of true humanity. When the mind is empty and still, it is also called the still small voice. If one does not listen to one's own still small voice, one simply adds one more layer of ignorance to one's own karma.

The still small voice, nevertheless, is generally thought of as something other than one's own true self. If that is the case, it means that one can never be truly honest to the voice. In relation to oneself, the voice will always be somewhat like the Greek monster, who kept an inn and insisted that all guests had to occupy the same-sized bed. If they were too long, he lopped off the excess. If they were too short, he stretched them. In other words, if pure consciousness or conscientiousness is thought of as altogether different from one's true self, its relationship to oneself must necessarily be Procrustean. If one has been taught that one should be able to give one's unqualified assent to the tiny small voice which is other than oneself, then when one finds that one is not able to do so, one shall inevitably feel sinful.

Many religions of the world and western religions in particular may be accused of manufacturing the very sense of sin of which they try to cleanse humans. One must always feel sinful when one tries to do something which is absolutely impossible, namely, when one tries to make oneself over in accordance with the will of another, even if that other is God. One will never be rid of the sense of sin until one recognizes two things: that individuality has ultimate rights and that the deepest truth cannot be one which asks humans to eliminate or suppress one's own individuality. The living truth must somehow also express one's individuality. It cannot do so unless one has a hand in shaping it. One can never with perfect sincerity bow to a God who is other than one's true self. Many traditional religions have never fully faced up to the full implications of this fact.

Case LXX. Simply Profound Or Profoundly Simple Truth

A student of Dao should have a right mind in order to take simplicity and truth as the basis of life. With a gourd and a piece of clothing, one can be at ease wherever one goes.

Xishan's Commentary

Buddha said, "The mind should be like a straight bowstring." He said again, "The straightforward mind is just the place for studying the way." If one is not attached to this body, one can be at ease wherever one travels.

Blowing Rock's Commentary

The right mind is the soul or the center of one's true self. It has nothing to do with the rigidity of one's own mind. The straightforward mind results neither from willful action nor from idle meditation. It has an easy, relaxed, effortless, or flowing quality. It is the place for the life of simplicity and truth. And thus it is the real temple of Buddha. The visible external temple is not a real place for meditation. In order to make no mistake about the nature of the straightforward mind, it has to be emphasized that the inner sanctuary is nothing but the place for gracefulness. Gracefulness is directly opposed both to rigidity and to flaccidity. It is rather supple strength or yielding power.

In oriental countries, the bamboo is regarded as the symbol of the straight mind and the model of what a personality should be. The oak tree is apparently more straight and stronger. However, it opposes the wind directly and fights the typhoon with the determination to remain upright. When the typhoon has blown over, the oak tree is often overturned. The bamboo bends before the wind. When the typhoon has blown itself out, the bamboo is still upright and standing.

This kind of pliant strength is the meaning of "the straightfoward mind." It can never come when one is doing from one's moral nature nor when one is driven by one's impulsive nature. It comes only from a truthful relationship with life. In other words, one is living from the soul or the center of one's true self. Gracefulness is withheld only when one's relationship to life is not truthful. Grace comes from God or from Buddha.

All doctrines, dogmas, and all ideas are human-made. That is why people who conform themselves to these stuffs are stern, narrow, and hard. It is for this reason that moralists, theologians, and all the host of people who are trying to subdue the body to the rigid mind are so often lacking in the gracefulness, that is, a right mind. They are crooked, twisted, complicated, articulated, sophisticated, contrived, and bent. Gracefulness means that one is filled by grace and acts with grace. Grace comes only so far as one is leading the life of a traveler, who is well at ease. A person of God or a student of Dao is necessarily a graceful person. One will have the softness of heart. If one wants a symbol of the truly upright personality, keep in mind the image of the lovely green flexible bamboo.

Case LXXI. The True Law

An ordinary person is absorbed in the actual things, while a student of Dao is absorbed in the ideal mind. Nevertheless, it is the true law that one should cast off both the actual and the ideal.

Xishan's Commentary

One who is absorbed in the actual things is like a thirsty deer who mistakes a heat wave for water and seeks for the heat haze. One who is absorbed in the ideal mind is like a monkey who mistakes a reflected moon in the water for the moon and tries to catch the reflected moon. Although the actual is different from the ideal, both are diseased. This speaks about both ordinary people and the two Vehicles.

Xishan's Poem

Heaven and earth have no Qin's sun and moon.
Hills and rivers have no Han's ruler and the ruled.

Blowing Rock's Commentary

Both the actual and the ideal have appealed to humans either simultaneously or alternately. The history of human thought oscillates endlessly among theories which would favor one or the other. So there have been partisans of realism and idealism. Some people, at times, lean towards either realistic world or idealistic Buddhism. They have vacillated between the two. The actual and the ideal are in opposition to one another, as Qin Dynasty is in opposition to Han Dynasty. At best, they are half the truth. At worst, they are diseased, that is, they have a lack of ease.

The quality of the enlightened person can flow neither from the realistic nor from the idealistic, because neither can muster the endorsement of the whole being of a person. In enlightenment, the actual and the ideal have been integrated: The world and the human have been married. Then one has no priority over the other. They are in need of one another. The actual without the ideal is blind, as meditation without wisdom is blind. The ideal without the actual is empty, as wisdom without meditation is abstract. In the authentic enlightenment, the actual has shaped the ideal as much as the ideal has shaped the actual. The ideal is not a preexistent pattern which has been imposed on an antecedent matter. If the ideal is a preexistent form, it would require a forcing. In that case, the actual matter would be provoked to some resistance. Nor does the ideal merely tag along after matter, which has been given free rein. In that case, it would make for incoherence. Wherever authentic enlightenment has been affected, the actual and the ideal have merged in a state of oneness. There is a Korean poem concerning this state of living oneness:

Desiring to catch the moon,
A monk ladled it out with the water into a vessel,
But, reaching the temple with it, found
That when he poured the water out, the moon was gone.

Case LXXII. Sitting Secluded In The Forest

Although a listener of Buddha's teaching sits secluded in the forest, one is caught by the devils. Although a Bodhisattva takes a stroll in the world, one is not seen by either pagans or a band of devils.

Xishan's Commentary

The mind wobbles, because a listener of Buddha's words regards stillness as the exercise of austerity. Whenever the mind wobbles, the devils can see it. On the other hand, a Bodhisattva does not leave any traces behind, because a Bodhisattva realizes that one's nature is originally empty and calm. Without traces left behind, pagans and the band of devils cannot see the Bodhisattva. This speaks about both the two Vehicles and the Bodhisattva.

Xishan's Poem

Taking a stroll down a flowery road in a spring breeze,
A certain house stands somberly in the rain.

Blowing Rock's Commentary

Whenever one considers a secluded place as the special condition for the enlightenment, one's mind is divorced from one's original nature, which is nothing but Buddha nature. In other words, one who tries to listen to the words of Buddha is not the Buddha. The listener exists independently of the Buddha. In another word, the listener's mind is crowded with external things such as the Buddha, his teachings, and the forest. One has an external relationship to them. Furthermore, the listener sitting secluded in the forest is totally isolated from people walking in the bustling world. These external things make a crowd. Whenever one considers Buddha or his teachings or the forest as a third thing alongside of one's own self and one's own life, then the third thing interferes with one's total life. Therefore, one has to decide to give priority to any one of them; either taking a stroll in the bustling city or sitting secluded in the forest. To Bodhisattvas, human task is not to force one's own self or life to surrender to any particular place or person. To put it more clearly, Bodhisattvas are freely in the world but not of the world.

One cannot begin to achieve enlightenment until one faces up to this question: "How can Buddha not be an external thing standing alongside oneself and one's life?" Insofar as this problem is not encountered, one shall always wobble between the forest and the world, between Buddha as the speaker and oneself as a listener, between Buddha's teachings and one's own words.

Devil can easily be encountered, if one insists on a life of one's own on the outside. If one regards the forest as the only dwelling place of Buddha, the forest becomes the dwelling place of devils. If one really wants to see Buddha, one has to die to one's attachment to any form of externality. Every blade of grass, every brook, every bird, every animal, every tree, or every thing in the forest asks humans to die to their externality and join in its life. Only through this death, one enters into enlightenment. Only through this renunciation of one's attachment to the external stillness, things become alive for oneself. Whenever one insists on preserving oneself as a listener of Buddha's words and on maintaining a separated existence, one lives an alienated life. And then the whole world around oneself is only an alien object. Then one's relationship to each one of them is external, abstract, and not truthful.

The dwelling place of Buddha is limited neither to *the Sutras* nor to the secluded forest. Buddha dwells wherever one lets him in. One lets him in, just when one lets go of one's externality. A Zen teacher was walking with his pupil in the country. The pupil said, "Sir, where may one enter the truth?" The teacher replied, "Do you hear the sound of the brook?" "Yes," said the disciple. The teacher answered, "There you may enter." If the sound is just an objective sound, then Buddha doesn't dwell there. Truth does not dwell there. It is something separate from the human. But if one can enter the sound to become one with the sound, then one touches its reality and thus its infinity. Only then one discovers where Buddha dwells.

Case LXXIII. Facing Death

Whenever one faces death, one should observe the following: The five skandhas are empty, so there is no I; the true mind has no form, so it neither goes nor comes; one's nature does not come to be, when one is born; one's nature does not go away, when one dies; one's nature is exceedingly bright and calm, so the mind and the environment are one. If one observes them as such and realizes them instantly, one will not be attached or attracted to the triple world and the law of causation. Such a one is distinctly a free human being in the world. Though one meets the Buddha, there is no mind to follow him. Though one sees the hell, there is no mind to fear. When one has no mind, one becomes equal to Fajie. This is the essential point. Therefore, every day is the cause, while last moment is the effect. Seekers should pay attention to this.

Xishan's Commentary

When one is afraid of dying and is in one's old age, one wishes to become intimately acquainted with the Buddha!

Xishan's Poem

Awake oneself this very moment,
One hundred years is but a flash.

Blowing Rock's Commentary

The five skandhas are body, perception, ideation, predisposition, and feeling. The term "skandha" means "to cover," "to be accumulated," or "to conglomerate." It is usually translated as "sheath." It explains both the elements of the universe and the structures of humankind.

Fajie (Dharmadatu in Sanskrit) means everything in the world, both material and immaterial. When one lets one's ego go, one becomes everything in the world. When the human mind is not separated from the world, then one touches infinity. Rather one becomes infinity found in every finite thing by way of entering into the union with one's own task, then every action is endowed with unbounded significance. So long as one does not become one with one's own task, no matter how dutifully one performs it, it will not be a holy union but merely a chore. As soon as one enters into any element of life without holding anything of oneself back on the outside, the finite is transfigured and becomes the Garden of Eden.

A Chinese saying goes, "When one is lured to fame and wealth, one becomes intimately acquainted with Confucius, while one is afraid of dying and is in one's old age, one becomes intimately acquainted with the Buddha." Zen, however, says that neither Confucianism nor Buddhism is the same thing as the essence of Zen Buddhism. The essence of Zen is union with life. The union of life is neither Confucian activity nor Buddhist passivity. Zen is the union with anything that life offers. Zen does what can be done when it can be done. And Zen lets the rest go and accepts the whole thing as it is.

Case LXXIV. A Hair's Breath Of Distinction

Even if the thought of a hair's breadth of distinction between sage and commoner remains at one's last moment, one will easily be dragged into the womb of an ass or that of a horse. Furthermore, one will be thrown into the hell of the boiling cauldron or be born as an ant or a mosquito.

Xishan's Commentary

Master Baiyun (?–1072 A. D.) said: "Even though there is no thought of a hairbreadth distinction between sage and commoner, it will be unavoidable for one to enter the womb of an ass or that of a horse." If the dualistic opinions flare up, many ways enter one's head.

Xishan's Poem

Burning fire flares out,
A treasured sword flashes forth!

Xishan's Further Commentary

Especially, Zen masters taught the two verses. When one has no mind, a door to the unity of the Dao will be opened. But for expediency's sake, one may also seek to be born in nirvana by chanting the name of Buddha. However, since every person's nature, capacity, intention, and desire are different, the two things are not opposed to each other. I wish for a student of Dao to do one's best within one's own capacity daily and have no doubts or regrets at one's last moment.

Blowing Rock's Commentary

Whether one makes a distinction between the enlightened and the unenlightened *or not,* both do originate from dualistic mind: One is opposed to the other. And thus a person is attached to one or the other. Both are the products of the conflict within oneself. The conflict produces doubt within one's mind. Doubt comes from the double mind. A mind, which is in two pieces, cannot be a mind at peace. One's thought of not making a distinction between the sacred and the secular is the suppression of one's thought of making distinction between A and not A. Therefore, it cannot be a basis of any kind of absolute peace. The reason that one has to suppress is because one doubts. The suppression is the covering up of the doubt or the pushing of the doubt to the rear of one's mind. The doubt is still there. The unenlightened are people who suppress. The heart of Zen is the way of the peace that passes understanding. What is a solution? How can anyone go beyond the two views? Is there a solution within the framework posed by the dualism? Or must the dualistic view be thrown out with the problem? In other words, can it be that the problem admits no solution in its own terms, but dissolution?

Therefore, the real problem is the dualism itself: that is, the forgetfulness of the non-arising place. The real solution would not come from perpetuating the dichotomy by an opting either for one or the other or for a middle position, but from relating to no mind where there is non-separation to begin with and which poses no such problem from the start. Dualism must be thrown into burning fire that is aflame. Dualism must be healed by the treasured sword which flashes. Right there the two are no longer opposed to each other.

More certainly than many things written in the Buddhist *Sutras*, Siddhartha Gautama Buddha went to the bathroom. This action of his is no less sacred and no more meaningful than the teaching of the Four Noble Truths. Because of the hardness of human hearts, Buddhists are taught to consider his first sermon as the holiest of all. To Zen, everything is holy as it is. *Every day is a good day*. Every moment is the best moment. And thus, one's everyday mind is the way. Walking, eating, sleeping, or playing is the way. The enlightened enjoy such a perfect freedom in all situations. One of the verses from the *Chanlinjuji* expresses such a perfect freedom:

Ride your horse along the edge of a sword;
Hide yourself in the middle of the flames.

Case LXXV. One's Original Face

If a Zen student does not see one's original face, how can one pass through the lofty front door of the mystery? Some take the emptiness of extinction as Zen. Some take the emptiness of inscrutability as the way. And others take the nonbeing of everything as the highest view. All these are dark hollowness and serious diseases. Nowadays how many people are there under the sun, who speak of Zen and do not suffer from such diseases?

Xishan's Commentary

The door, which is facing upward, has no foothold. Master Yunmen said: "If one does not pierce through the light, two kinds of sickness arise; Even though one pierces through the Dharmakaya, two kinds of sickness also come into being; One should begin to pierce through them all one at a time."

Xishan's Poem

Without walking along the thick grassy road,
It is difficult to reach the flower-scattered village!

Blowing Rock's Commentary

One's original face is one's true self. It is most needful to realize the truth that no genuine spiritual freedom can be achieved by being oblivious of one's true self. Nowadays so many people look upon Zen Buddhism as a bundle of general or objective truths wrapped together by Zen masters in the orient. They hope to make themselves truthful by taking part in a kind of institutional ownership of the package of truth. Nevertheless, no one can authenticate one's identity by adhering to Zen Buddhism, which is other than one's true self.

A Zen teacher asked Yunmen (864–949 A. D.) to speak anything of Zen. He could not say anything. The teacher threw him out of the front door. One foot of his was caught in the door. And his toes were bleeding. At that very moment, he was enlightened. In one of his preaching, Yunmen said: "There are two kinds of sickness if one does not pierce through the light; The first is that there seems to be something in front of one's eye; The second is that one still has a dim picture of some existence even after one knows the principle of emptiness; there are still two other kinds of disease, even after one pierces through the Body of Law (Dharmakaya); The first is either that one is adhered to the Body of Law or that one maintains one opinion of this Law. The second is that there still remains some forms of life. The Dharmakaya is the same as One Thing mentioned in the first case. It is always bright and holy. It does not have any history. It is beyond expression.

Joshu began the study of Zen when he was sixty years old and continued the study until he was eighty, when he realized Enlightenment. He taught Zen until he was 120. One day a student asked him: "If I have emptiness in my mind, what then shall I do?" Joshu replied: "Throw the emptiness out." The student continued: "But if I have nothing, how can I throw it out?" "Well," said Joshu, "then carry it out." Even when there is nothing left in one's mind, there is the emptiness which stands between the pupil and his true self. It is likened to a food particle, which gets in between the teeth. The attachment to emptiness becomes one of the greatest barriers to real enlightenment. For the majority of Zen people today there is either an unawareness of this sickness, that is, attachment to emptiness, or there is a kind of hypocritical pretense that enlightenment has been achieved.

Case LXXVI. Many Kinds Of Disease

Patriarchs also have many kinds of disease. Those who are ill at ease with their ears and eyes regard Zen as making their eyes glare, giving ears, and nodding their heads. Those who are ill at ease with their tongues and mouths regard Zen as talking at random and making belly shouts (katz) indiscriminately. Those who are ill at ease with their hands and feet regard Zen as moving backward and forward, and pointing east and west. Those who are ill at ease with their hearts-and-stomachs regard Zen as seeking after subtle things or researching for curious things, leaving passions and opinions behind. However, truly speaking, there is not a single thing that is not diseased.

Xishan's Commentary

One who kills one's parent can repent before Buddha. However anyone who slanders prajna has no way to repent.

Xishan's Poem

How absurd it is to catch shadows in the empty air,
What is so splendid about leaping out of the world?

Blowing Rock's Commentary

An enlightened person can find oneself in no situation where one is not at ease with oneself. Being-not-at-ease-with means disease. Disease is lack of ease. When any part of a human being attempts to capture or control one's own being, one is not at ease with oneself. The root of many kinds of disease lies in the division between mind and body. Both body and mind are parts of a human being. Zen does not call upon oneself to destroy any one of them. Instead it asks oneself to root both body and mind in life itself so that both body and mind may be the expression and the servant of life.

Zen is nothing special. It is not a special possession. It has to be everything or nothing. It is not a special teaching. It is not limited to a special part of oneself. So long as one withholds any part of oneself from any living task, one has to remain external to life itself. Whenever one remains external to life, one's body will be external to one's mind and *vice versa*. If one closes one's eyes and looks at oneself from the inside, one can say that one is a mind. One has feelings, ideas, and desires. One can just feel them inside. This is an inside to oneself. This inside Xishan calls "hearts-and-stomachs." Philosophers call it mind: It has no particular shape, no weight, and no color. One cannot touch it. Then there is also an outside which one calls one's body which consists of ears, eyes, tongue, mouth, hands, and feet: One can touch, weigh, measure, and sense it. In this way, one is split between body and mind. This split corresponds to the distinction between the ideal and the actual that Xishan mentioned in the earlier case.

There are enlightened persons who are not afflicted with this division. Such people are living wholly. They do not know themselves as divided between mind and body. They do not have any problem of uniting mind and body. They are at ease with themselves. For these people, there is no need to focus on a specific part of oneself in order to practice Zen. To them, there is no place where Buddha can be hidden. Buddha cannot hold itself back. Buddha cannot be just something either on the inside or on the outside. Whenever one is liberated from dualism of mind and body, one has achieved spiritual freedom.

Spiritual freedom produces an adjustment to life in its infinite way. Adjustment to life is not an adjustment to a limited area of life. It cannot be based on a system. It is not an adjustment of the mind or the body but an adjustment of the spirit. Herein lies the difference between wisdom (prajna) and knowledge. Knowledge is always definite and finite. Wisdom, however, must be something infinitely flexible in order to be true to life in its infinite nature. A real adjustment is of spirit. The more free one's adjustment to life is, the more it is a trusting of the spirit and a withdrawing from reliance on knowledge. Such an adjustment of the spirit can be called wisdom-Zen or Zen-wisdom. Wisdom without Zen is discriminating knowledge. Zen without wisdom is empty and blind. Zen-wisdom or wisdom-Zen is called "Prajna."

Case LXXVII. The Phrases Of Authentic Masters

The phrases of authentic masters are likened to the clapping and singing of an idiot, snow on a hot oven, or a flash of lightning; students of Dao cannot make any sense out of them. Therefore, a man of old said gratefully to his teacher: "I do not respect my teacher's virtue, but admire him for not explaining things to me."

Xishan's Commentary

Don't speak out, Don't speak out, Unless one may put pen to paper!

Xishan's Poem

Shooting an arrow to pierce the moon reflected in the river,
He must be hunting for an eagle.

Blowing Rock's Commentary

Zen students are supposed to admire their teachers for not explaining the one thing needful to them. There is a Zen story, which makes this point in its own way. It teaches that one must not deprive a student of the supreme privilege of experiencing life for oneself by telling one what life is about or what Buddha is. In the Tang dynasty in China there was a monk by the name of Daowu who was deeply troubled with the problem of life and death, of being and nothing, and of good and evil. In particular, he was deeply concerned about death. He agonized over the question for a long time. One day he and his teacher, Jianyuan, went to a funeral. While they were there, Daowu knocked on the coffin and said, with his eyes begging for an answer, "Is he alive or is he dead?" Jianyuan replied, "I do not say he is alive, I do not say he is dead." "Why won't you tell me?" asked Daowu. "I will not say, I will not say." replied the teacher. On the way home, the agitation continued in the monk's heart to the point where he turned to his teacher and said, "If you don't tell me, I'll strike you." The teacher said, "As to striking me, that's your affair, but as for me, I will not say. I will not say." The monk was so overwrought that he struck his teacher, but still he could extract no answer from him. Some time went by and the boy continued his search, and then his teacher died. He went to the teacher's eldest disciple, Shishuang and repeated the same question, "Is he alive or is he dead?"

Shishuang said, "I do not say he is alive. I do not say he is dead." "I beg you to tell me." Implored the monk. "I will not say. I will not say." The eldest disciple replied. The monk suddenly realized the truth. That is, he grasped the reality of life and death in a way that he never could have in an answer given him by another. It was then he understood the enormous kindness of his teacher in not supplying him with an abstract answer but forcing him to go on to the very end of his existential quest.

Case LXXVIII. Zen Belly Shout

First of all, students should know the various schools of Zen in detail. Long ago, when master Mazu uttered one Zen belly shout, "katz," master Baizhang was deafened while master Huangbo put out his tongue. This katz is not only the message of Buddha's lifting the flower but also the face of Bodhidharma's first coming. This becomes the origin of Linji school.

Xishan's Commentary

Being afraid of one who knows the law. Strike a person who utters a sound.

Xishan's Poem

A staff, having not a single joint,
Stealthily is given to a traveler at night.

Xishan's Further Commentary

Long ago, with Mazu's katz, Baizhang attained the great potentiality while Huangbo attained the great function. The great potentiality is a universal adjustment to life. The great function is a straight cutting. This is recorded in *The Record of the Transmission of the Lamp*.

Blowing Rock's Commentary

Mazu was born in 709 A. D., and died in 788 A. D. at the age of 80. One day, master Nanyu Huairang asked Mazu, "what are you doing?" He replied, "I sit and meditate." The master asked again, "What is the purpose of sitting meditation?" He also replied, "I want to become Buddha." Next day, the master came and sat beside Mazu. And he began to polish a tile before Mazu. Mazu asked the master, "Sir, why are you polishing the tile?" The master replied, "I will make a mirror out of it." Mazu retorted, "How can you make a mirror out of a tile?" The master caught the moment and said, "Is that so? Likewise, can the sitting meditation make you become Buddha?" At this, Mazu was awakened. And he begged the master, "Then what shall I do?" The master answered, "When a cart does not move, should one whip the cart or the cow?"

"Likewise, Zen has nothing to do with sitting or lying." "Buddha does not dwell in calm place." "Zen is nothing but non-attachment, and it is neither mere activity nor mere passivity." At this, Mazu was greatly enlightened.

Baizhang was born in 720 A.D., and died in 814 A.D. His enlightenment, at the hands of Mazu, is told in the 53rd Case in *The Blue Cliff Record*. One day Mazu was walking in the country. Baizhang was with him. Both of them heard the sound of some wild ducks. Mazu said, "What kind of sound is it?" Baizhang replied, "it is the sound of wild ducks." Mazu said, "Where is the sound?" Baizhang answered, "The sound has gone." Mazu twisted Baizhang's nose. And he painfully cried out. Mazu asked, "Will you still say that it has gone?"

The next day when Mazu was on the pulpit to start preaching, Baizhang rolled up the prayer rug. Mazu immediately came down and went back to his room. Later Mazu said to Baizhang, "What is the meaning of rolling up the prayer rug even before I began to preach?" Baizhang said, "Yesterday you wrenched my nose, and it really hurt." Mazu asked, "Where did you focus your mind yesterday?" Baizhang replied, "My nose does not hurt today."

Later in his life, Mazu uttered a katz which made Baizhang deaf and blind for three days. During these days, Baizhang *passively* learned how to adjust himself to all kinds of situations in life. And he attained the great potentiality. One of his famous sayings is "A day of no working is a day of no eating." It was Baizhang who first reformed regulations of the Zen temples nearly three centuries after the coming of Bodhidharma.

The date of Huangbo's birth is not recorded, but he died in 850 A.D. When Baizhang told Huangbo a story about his own enlightenment experience caused by Mazu, Huangbo *actively* displayed the great function by sticking out his tongue. The great potentiality like Buddha's lifting of a flower is the passive aspect of Zen, while the great function like Bodhidharma's coming to China is the active side of Zen. One day Huangbo visited Baizhang. Baizhang asked him, "Where did you come from?" Huangbo answered, "I came from The Stately Way." Baizhang said, "What did you come here for?" Huangbo answered, "Nothing special." Baizhang recognized his enlightenment.

The Record of the Transmission of the Lamp was originally written by Yongan Daoyuan. Later it was admitted into the complete collections of the Buddhist *Sutras* in 1004 A.D. It is a collection of the sayings and lives of many Zen masters in China.

Case LXXIX. Linji School

There are five schools in patriarchal Zen: Linji (Linzai in Japanese) school, Caodong (Soto in Japanese) school, Yunmen (Unmon in Japanese) school, Weiyang (Igyo in Japanese) school, and Fayan (Hogen in Japanese) school.

Linji School:
The following masters directly followed the line of the sixth patriarch Huineng who was a thirty-third patriarch from our teacher, Sakyamuni Buddha:
Nanyu Huairang (677–744 A.D.), Mazu Daoyi (709–788 A.D.), Baizhang Huaihai (720–814 A.D.), Huangbo Xiyun (?–850 A.D.), Linji Yixian (?–867 A.D.), Xinghua Cunjiang (?–925 A.D.), Nanyuan Daoyong (?), Fengxue Yanzhao (896–937 A.D.), Shoushan Shengnian (926–993 A.D.), Fengyang Shanzhao (947–1024 A.D.), Ciming Chuyuan (987–1040 A.D.), Yangqi Fanghui (992–1049 A.D.), Baiyun Shouduan (?–1072 A.D.), Wuzu Fayan (?–1104 A.D.), Yuanwu Keqin (1063–1135 A.D.), and Jingshan Zonggao (1089–1163 A.D.)

Blowing Rock's Commentary

Before Sakyamuni Buddha entered nirvana, Buddha as the first patriarch selected Mahakasyapa to whom he transmitted the Dharma. And he gave his robe as insignia of his authority and his spiritual attainment. There are twenty-eight patriarchs in the orthodox line of transmission in India. They are as follows:

1. Sakyamuni
2. Mahakasyapa
3. Ananda
4. Sanavasa
5. Upagupta
6. Dhritika
7. Micchaka
8. Buddhanandi
9. Buddhamitra
10. Bhikshu Parsva
11. Punyayasas
12. Asvaghosha

13. Bhikshu Kapimala
14. Nagarjuna
15. Kanadeva
16. Arya Rahulata
17. Samghanandi
18. Samghayasas
19. Kumaralata
20. Jayata
21. Vasubandhu
22. Manura
23. Haklenayasas
24. Bhikshu Simha
25. Vasasita
26. Punyamitra
27. Prajnatara
28. Bodhidharma

Bodhidharma as the twenty-eighth patriarch in India came to China around 520 A. D., he became the first patriarch of Zen in China. There are five patriarchs after him:

1. Bodhidharma or Dharma
2. Huike or Eka in Japanese (487–593 A.D.)
3. Sengchan or Sosan in Japanese (died 606 A.D.)
4. Daoxin or Doshin in Japanese (580–651 A.D.)
5. Hongren or Konin in Japanese (602–675 A.D.)
6. Huineng or Eno in Japanese (638–713 A.D.)

Xinghua Cunjiang used to say: "There is not a single enlightened person in Southern China, who can be caught by a Zen stick." He loved Linji, because Linji is neither too cold nor too kind. Other masters were either so kind to provide external Zen answers to unprepared students or too indifferent to help students. So Xinghua made up his mind to follow the line of Linji school or house, because he understood the enormous kindness of Linji hidden behind Linji's harsh teaching methodology in not supplying him with an abstract answer but in helping him to go on to the very end of his existential quest.

Nanyuan Daoyong asked Fengxue, "What do you think of Zen stick from southern China?" Fengxue Yanzhao answered, "It is commendable." And he continued to ask, "What about Zen stick here?"

Daoyong lifted his Zen stick and said, "people under the Zen stick are unable to see the teacher." At this phrase, Fengxue was enlightened. One day, Fengxue Yanzhao cried out. Monks were surprised and asked him the reason why he cried. He explained, "Why in the world is the line of Linji school going to be terminated by me!" At this moment, Nienfahua begged, "Can I receive dharma from you?" Fengxue answered, "But it is a pity that you are caught by *the Sutras*." Nienfahua retorted, "Is it alright if I discard *the Sutras*?" Fengxue responded, "Of course!" And he became enlightened at later period of time. One day, Fengxue said during his sermon, "What do you think of Sakyamuni Buddha's looking at Mahakasyapa?" "I will bury the Buddha, if you think of his looking at Mahakasyapa merely as a sign of the recipient of his special transmission without words." At this moment, Soushan Shengnian attained the great enlightenment and left in the middle of the sermon.

Fenyang Shanzhao studied Zen under Soushan. One day, Soushan said in his sermon, "Wherever an elephant steps, the trace of a fox is erased." Fengyang was enlightened at this phrase.

Ciming Chuyuan studied under Fenyang Shanzhao who used to use cursing and dirty words instead of giving dharma speech. One day, Ciming asked Fenyang to teach dharma in a decent manner. He was mad at him, saying, "Do you criticize me?" And he chased Ciming out. As soon as Ciming started to explain, Fenyang stopped up Ciming's mouth with his fist. And Ciming was enlightened.

Yangqi Fanghui was a head monk who worked for Ciming. Wuzu Fayan was enlightened by the yelling sound of Baiyun Shouduan. And then he wrote the following Zen dialogue or poem:

> I ask an old man, "Why do you enjoy the old and tiny portion of land located under the mountain so much?" The old man says, "I sold it, but the reason why I bought it back again is the clean wind in the bamboo grove and pine trees."

When somebody asked Wuzu a question, "What is the birth place of Buddha?" Wuzu answered, "Home is cool, when the wind blows." At this answer, Yuanwu Keqin was enlightened. Jingshan Zonggao received Dharma from Yuanwu Keqin. And he emphasized the gong'an method instead of just sitting meditation.

Case LXXX. Caodong School

Caodong School is a branch from the line of the sixth patriarch Huineng, and had the following masters:
Qingyuan Xingsi, Shitou Xiqian, Yaoshan Weiyan, Yunyan Tancheng, Dongshan Liangji, Caoshan Danzhang, and Yunju Daoying.

Blowing Rock's Commentary

The origin of this school or house is not known. "Cao" is derived from Caoshan, while "Dong" is derived from Dongshan. Caoshan is the disciple of Dongshan. The family tradition of this Zen house is based on the non-duality of word and action, and that of the actual and the ideal. Since Linji School has considered itself as orthodox house of Zen, the rest of Zen houses are considered as branches (heterodoxy) of Zen School. However, In the spirit of Zen, there is no distinction between the orthodox and the heterodox. Qingyuan Xingsi (?–740 A.D.), for example, was the chief disciple of the sixth patriarch Huineng. Therefore, it is simply wrong to say that Caodong School is merely a branch of Zen house. There is an interesting story about him. A monk asked Qingyuan, "What is the meaning of Bodhidharma's coming to China?" He answered, "He went off again somewhere." The monk then said, "I beg you for short words of wisdom." Qingyuan said, "Come here!" The monk came closer. Qingyuan said, "Write it down clearly."

Shitou Xiqian (700–790 A. D.) had a wild character: He broke down the evil customs practiced by the superstitious people in his town. After he left his home town, he served the sixth patriarch, Huineng. By the sixth patriarch's will, he visited Qingyuan Xingsi, under whom Shitou was enlightened.

Yaoshan Weiyan (the eighth century A.D.) was originally a student of *the Sutras*. One day he came to realization and said, "Why should a brave man be tied down to the written law!? Just purify oneself." And he went to see Shitou (Sekito) and was enlightened. However, he left Shitou to see Mazu and stayed there for three years. Again he returned to Shitou and continued to spread Shitou's teaching.

Yunyan Tancheng (782–841 A.D.) served Baizhang Huaihai for twenty years as an attendant. After Baizhang died, he went to serve Yaoshan. One day Dongshan Liangji (807–869 A.D.) met Yunyan and said, "According to master Huizhong, even inanimate things preach the sermons, who will listen to them?" Yunyan answered, "Inanimate things are listening to the sermons." Then he asked, "Do you listen to their sermons too?" Yunyan retorted, "If I listen, you will not be able to listen to my sermons." At this, he was awake. One day, Dongshan was crossing a river, he saw his own shadow reflected on the river. He was greatly enlightened and understood Yunyan's words. Right before Yunyan dies, Dongshan asked him, "If someone wants to see you after your death, what should I do?" Yunyan answered, "Just say, 'It is just like this.'" At this answer, Dongshan silently lowered his head. Having made a long pause, Yunyan continued to answer, "You must think through this principle." Again Dongshan was crossing a river, he was suddenly enlightened and understood Yunyan's words. And he thanked him for not explaining the meaning of the statement, "It is just like this." (See Case LXXVII.)

Caoshan Danzhang (839–901 A.D.) was well versed with Confucian books. At the age of nineteen, he left his home to study Zen under Dongshan. However, his line of Zen house did not continue after four generations.

There is an interesting story about Yunju Daoying (?–902 A.D.): Yunju had not taken the regular meals for ten days. On the tenth day, he visited the kitchen and he was asked by Dongshan, "What happened?" He answered, "I have been fed by the gods of heaven." Dongshan said, "I thought you have had a right-minded view, but you had a small-minded view." And Dongshan continued to probe him, "What is it when you think of neither good nor bad?" By this question, he was enlightened. Since then, the gods of heaven never appeared to him again. One day, Yunju sent a pair of pants to a head monk of a temple. The monk refused to receive it by saying, "I received Nirvana-clothes since my birth." Yunju asked the monk, "What did you wear before you were born?" The monk could not answer. After the monk died, somebody brought his relic left from the cremation. Yunju drily commented, "What is the value of the relic, since he failed to answer my question?"

Case LXXXI. Yunmen School

Yunmen School is a branch of Mazu (Baso). And had the following masters:

Tianwang Daowu, Longtan Chongxin, Deshan Xuanjian, Xuefeng Yicun, Yunmen Wenyan, Xuedou Zhongxian, and Tianyi Yihuai.

Blowing Rock's Commentary

Tianwang Daowu (748–807 A.D.) studied Zen from various masters. Among them were Mazu Daoyi and Shitou Xiqian. He spent two years under the influence of Mazu. At the age of thirty-four, however, he was greatly enlightened by Shitou. He spent ten years with Shitou. Right before Tianwang was about to die, he asked the head of a temple where he stayed, "Do you know?" The head monk said, "I do not know." At this answer, he threw his wooden pillow away and died.

The date of the birth and death of Longtan Chongxin is unknown. The literal meaning of "Longtan" means "dragon in the pond." When he was young, he used to bring ten pieces of rice cake made by his mother to master Daowu. The master always gave one piece of the rice cake back to Longtan. Longtan asked, "What is the meaning of returning one piece to me?" The master answered, "Is there anything wrong for me to return one piece back to you?" At this, Longtan made up his mind to leave his home for Zen training under the guidance of the master Daowu. One day he expressed his seeming failure in training Zen to his teacher: "I have been taking care of you for a long period of time, and yet you have not taught me the essence of Zen." The master retorted, "I have been teaching you since you came here: When you brought food, did not I eat it? When you brought tea, did not I drink it? When you made a bow to me, Did not I make a bow to you?" At this, he was enlightened. He asked him further, "How can I continue to keep it?" The master said, "Live freely according to your karma. And come and go as you like. There is no holy mind except getting rid of the ordinary mind."

Deshan Xuanjian (780–865 A.D.) was the master of teaching *the Diamond Sutras*. One day he said to his students, "It is said that a Bodhisattva can attain Buddhahood only through innumerable period of time. However, the southerners say that Buddhahood can instantly be attained merely through pointing to one's mind. I am going to correct them." And he left for the south. On the way, he entered into a restaurant, and ordered a piece of rice cake for his lunch. The old female owner of the restaurant asked him, "What is in your bag?" He answered with full of dignity, "*The commentary on the Diamond Sutra*." The old woman said, "According to *the Diamond Sutra*, 'there is no mind of past, no mind of present, and no mind of future.' 'Now you are going to take your lunch here, what kind of mind of yours is it?'" Deshan could not answer. At this, the old woman asked him to see master Longtan. Deshan went to find Longtan and said with pride, "There is neither the dragon nor the pond." Longtan responded by saying, "You indeed came to the dragon in the pond." Once again, he was unable to say anything at this remark. That night, he chatted and spent most of the night with the head priest. At last, he was about to leave for one of the guest rooms. It was pitch dark outside. As he came back in, the master handed him a candle light. As Deshan was about to receive the candle, the master blew it out. At this, Deshan was greatly enlightened. Deshan made a bow to Longtan. Longtan said, "Why do you make the bow to me?" Deshan answered, "From now on, I will never give any doubt to the sayings of masters." Next day, he burned *the Commentary on the Diamond Sutra*. And he continued to travel. Wherever he went, he abolished temples which contained Buddha statues except the sermon hall. As his teaching method, he used to use wooden staff to awaken his disciples.

Xuefeng Yicun (822–908 A.D.) studied Zen under many masters. However, Deshan's staff made him have a first enlightenment. Many Korean masters studied with him.

Xuedu Zhongxian (980–1052 A.D.) visited a Zen master and said, "What is the meaning of the statement that there is a great mistake even without a single line of thought?" The master asked him to come near him. As he came near him, the master struck him hard. As Xuedu tried to say something, the master again struck his mouth. At this, he was enlightened. As he was about to die, one of his disciples asked him to say a last word for them. He said, "I have spoken a lot during my life, that is my worry."

Tianyi Yihuai (989–1060 A.D.) was the son of a fisherman. As he followed his father to go fishing, he let living fish go. Having left his home, he served and studied under master Zhongxian. One day, master Zhongxian said, "It is not this, it is not that; it is not that it is neither this nor that." As soon as Tianyi tried to say something, the master immediately struck him. One day, he drew water from a well, suddenly he was greatly enlightened by the breaking sound of the frame for carrying water.

Case LXXXII. Weiyang School

Weiyang School as a branch of Baizhang had the following masters: Weishan Lingyou, Yangshan Huiji, Xiangyan Zhixian, Nanta Guangyong, Baijiao Huiqing, Huoshan Jingtong, and Wuzhi Wenxi.

Blowing Rock's Commentary

Although Xiangyan Zhixian was asked by his townspeople to become a government officer, he made up his mind to leave his home. And he went to a place where master Weishan stayed. Weishan asked him, "Say a phrase about the original face before you were born without quoting anything that you saw or heard before." He tried to answer the question in many different ways. All the answers of his were rejected. He was very dismayed, returned to his room, and tried to find an answer by reading books. He could not find any answer there. He went to see and beg the master to teach him. Weishan retorted, "My answer is my own: It is of no use to you." Having heard this, he burnt all of his books, and left Weishan. One day, he joined to help people who worked on a mountain. In the middle of work, he picked one pebble and threw it at the bamboo forest. At the sound of a pebble striking a bamboo, he was greatly enlightened. And he faced to the place where master Weishan lived and composed a poem: "I have forgotten everything at one sound of striking, no need for me to seriously cultivate myself again."

When Nanta Guangyong was born, strange light was filled in his birthplace. Horses in a nearby barn were startled and made a noise. That was the reason why his name Guangyong was given. Baijio Huiqing was a Korean master who was enlightened by the sermon given by master Nanta, and became Nanta's disciple. Huoshan Jingtong was a disciple of Yangshan. Yangshan used to teach his disciples by hitting four times with Zen stick. Before Huoshan was about to die, he collected dry firewood and was self-immolated by the fire. Wuzhi Wenxi (820–899 A.D.) left his home at the age of seven, and became one of Yangshan's disciples. When a Bodhisattva, Manjusri appeared from a cauldron where he cooked hot cereal, he made the following statements, "Manjusri is Manjusri, Wuzhi is Wuzhi: I am not concerned about this at all!" And he struck Manjusri with a large flat wooden spoon.

Case LXXXIII. Fayan School

Fayan School as a branch of Xuefeng had the following masters: Xuansha Shibei, Dizang Guichen, Fayan Wenyi, Tiantai Deshao, Yongming Yanshou, Longji Shaxu, and Nantai Shouan.

Blowing Rock's Commentary

Xuansha Shibei (835–908) left home at the age of thirty. He used to abstain from eating and practice the sitting meditation under the rocks or on the top of the mountains. He was enlightened of himself. A Korean Zen master by the name of Xueyue Lingguang studied under him.

Dizang Guichen (867–928) was a vegetarian. He ate one meal a day. However, he realized that asceticism was not the way of enlightenment. At the age of twenty he left home to learn from Xuefeng, who did not help him very much. So he left him and stayed with Xuansha Shibei by whom he was enlightened. Dizang loved to work at the rice field. One day Dizang was working at the rice field, he asked Longji Shaoxu who just came back from the south, "How is the southern Buddhism? Is it different from us who make rice?" Longji answered, "Not free from the three worlds yet!?" Dizang retorted, "What is this that you call the three worlds?" By this retort, he was suddenly enlightened. And he became one of the disciples of Dizang.

Fayan Wenyi left home at the age of seven. He studied the Buddhist precepts, Confucianism, and its poetry. He met Dizang who asked him many questions, but Fayan was not interested in answering him. When he was about to leave, Dizang asked, "The three worlds are the mind; is this stone within the mind or without?" He quickly answered, "It is within the mind." And Dizang said, "How can a monk continue to walk, while carrying a stone in his mind?" At this comment, he was dumbfounded. However, he decided to stay with Dizang, and expressed many opinions of his. Dizang, however, responded with a uniformed statement, "That is not the truth." Fayan finally confessed, "I have exhausted all my opinions." At this confession, Dizang said, "If you speak the truth, all things are true as they are." At this, he was enlightened. Nantai Shouan with two other monks from Korea studied under him.

Tiantai Deshao (891–972) left home at the age of eighteen. He was very disappointed in many Zen masters. And thus he made up his mind to stay with common monks. One day, a monk asked Fayan, "What is a drop of water originated from the valley of Caoci?" The master answered,

"This is the drop of water from the origin of Caoxi." By hearing this, Tiantai, who had sat at a corner of the room, was greatly enlightened. He followed the spirit of Fayan School.

Yongming Yanshou (904–975) left his home at the age of twenty-eight. He was one of the disciples of Tiantai Deshao. He was very fond of reciting *the Sutras* and of chanting Buddha's name innumerably.

Case LXXXIV. Zen Shout and Zen Stick

The thundering shout of Linji and the stick of Deshan thoroughly witness the way that has no birth and transparently penetrate through the eternal way from its top to its bottom. The great substance and the great function are so free that they are not caught by anything. Furthermore they appear and disappear with their whole bodies and carry loads on their whole bodies. And thus they protect the boundary of the sainthood just like Wenshu and Puxian. Nevertheless, truly speaking, these two masters (Linji and Deshan) will unavoidably become ghosts.

Xishan's Commentary

Don't touch the sharp edge of a knife.

Xishan's Poem

A gem is reflected on very bright shiny water,
The moon is passing through the unclouded blue sky!

Blowing Rock's Commentary

Linji began to create Zen-shout, that is, katz, while Deshan began to use Zen stick. Creative freshness about their methods is present only in the original beginning of Linji's shout and Deshan's stick. Later their disciples merely repeated and imitated teachers' tools. And thus they petrified both the freshness of shout and genuine surprise of staff into inauthentic formality. Therefore, to keep their fresh creativity is not to imitate them but to create new methods. If one wants Buddha nature or enlightenment, one has constantly in everything to begin anew. This is certainly not any kind of mere return to some static *Sutras* of the past, which is believed to enshrine the truth once and for all in some fixed mold. To begin anew means to open oneself creatively and fearlessly to the reality of each living situation, and to allow oneself to be taught by that reality.

Whatever else Zen method may be, it has got to be something that is intimately related to one's life as an individual. It cannot be simply a general or an objective method, simply because an objective method would not be rooted in one's own life and thus would not have the power to vivify oneself. The only method that can liberate individuals is one which is inseparable from one's own being. An objective method can be shared with others, and thus it is some kind of common property. As such, it cannot deliver one from one's personal bondage. The method that sets oneself free is thus not an external one but a method to be united with one's true self.

Enlightenment is not a separate goal to be achieved by certain methods. If the methods are not real, they cannot lead to enlightenment. If a shout is not real, it will not produce naturalness or freedom. In Zen one cannot separate the methods and the goals. Many of Zen seekers may be persuaded that they are deeply sincere seekers. They may be persuaded that they are faithfully following their teachers' methods to bring themselves to the goal. However, this is a false separation between ends and means. It is most needful to realize that in relation to Zen, that is, enlightenment, there are no external methods separated from one's self. Enlightenment is not gained by manipulating external methods but through giving up the externality. The more one learns to die to one's externality, the more one enters into enlightenment.

Case LXXXV. A Brave Person

A brave person should regard a Buddha or a patriarch as an enemy. If one is attached to the Buddha to ask for anything, one is bound by the Buddha. If one is attached to a patriarch to ask for anything, one is bound by the patriarch. Asking for anything is suffering. It is no better than having nothing to do.

Xishan's Commentary

The phrase, "A brave person should regard a Buddha or a patriarch as an enemy," is tied to the earlier phrase, "the stirring of ripples without wind." The phrase, "asking for anything is suffering," is tied to the previously mentioned phrase, "All is right as it is." The phrase, "It is no better than having nothing to do," is knotted to the previously mentioned phrase, "it goes awry as soon as one begins to think." If these things are done, the tips of tongues of all the people in the whole world will be cut from one's own seats. And the fast spinning wheel of samsara will come to a standstill of itself. Relieving people of their crises and restoring peace are likened to Danxia's burning of the wooden image of Buddha, or Yunmen's intending to feed dogs, or an old woman's having a dislike to see the Buddha. All these things are means to get rid of things that are wicked in order to reveal things that are righteous. In the end, what shall one do?

Xishan's Poem

Always longing for March in the south of the river,
Where partridges sing and a hundred flowers smell sweet.

Blowing Rock's Commentary

A brave person is one who has courage to be. A courageous person does not follow the footsteps of Siddhartha Gautama Buddha but does create one's own path. When Siming, a Korean saintly teacher, visited Xishan, Xishan asked him, "Where did you come from?" Siming answered, "I came here by following the old traditional way." Xishan shouted to him, "Do not follow the old way." At this moment, Siming realized the meaning of the shout. Zen Buddhism in China began to introduce creative changes into the existing Buddhist community, which Gautama Buddha might have carried out. Many people including Buddhists may not understand the real intention of Zen Buddhism, although Zen Buddhism has been doing exactly as The Buddha did. Namely, Gautama Buddha imitated no one and, therefore, Zen masters urged their students to imitate no one. Likewise, Xishan asked Siming not to imitate the traditional way. In this sense, both Xishan and Siming were real followers of Buddha. Indeed, this is the only way to imitate the founder of Buddhism. And that is not to imitate Buddha.

Seen from this point of view, a really brave person is neither a teacher whom one can imitate nor a master who urges others to imitate. The brave wants others to be themselves, that is, to create. Of course, one should absorb something of the spirit of the brave persons. However, if one attempts to achieve other's enlightenment by imitating the other, one will never be anything but an epigone. As Zen says, "counting other people's money does not make you rich."

Danxia (739–828 A. D.) traveled around the world. One wintry night, he entered a Buddhist temple. It was so cold and could not find any kindling to start fire to warm him up. He found that the Buddha image in the sermon hall was made out of wood. He brought out the wooden Buddha image. He chopped the image with an axe to make some kindling out of it. The head monk of the temple was very angry at this apparent blasphemous behavior. Danxia dug out ashes with a stick, and muttered to himself, "Where in the world are Buddha's bones? I could not find them yet." The head monk commented, "How in the world do you expect to find Buddha's bones from a wooden image?" Danxia responded, "Without his bones, it is not the Buddha but a piece of wood." Danxia used this method to get rid of the image of Buddha in order to reveal the real Buddha.

It was reported that Siddhartha Gautama said right after he was born, "I am alone in the whole world." Yunmen Wenyan commented on this saying, "If I were there with him, I would have killed him with a stick to feed the hungry dogs to restore peace." At this comment, many enlightened persons said, "It is Yunmen who really explained the true meaning of the Buddha's saying, he is truly Buddha's disciple." One of Oscar Wilde's aphorisms asserts that the truth ceases to be true when more than one person believes in it. For Yunmen, the truth ceases to be true even when one person believes in it.

When the historical Buddha came to a town to preach a sermon, a multitude came to listen to him. However, an old woman stayed at home and locked the door. She covered her eyes with her fingers in order not to see the Buddha. However, the Buddha revealed himself through the tips of all her fingers. This anecdote teaches that all beings have their Buddha nature. It is a form of ignorance for the multitude to see or hear the Buddha externally, since no one can escape from one's own Buddha nature. The closing of one's eyes, the opening of one's eyes, the lifting of one's finger, tips of one's fingers, the staying at one's home, the locking of one's door, or the disliking to see the Buddha can all be the appearance of the Buddha.

If those things are just limited human actions, the Buddha, of course, does not dwell there. But if one's action is wholehearted, then one can find the Buddha in one's own action. For example, if one's own asking is wholehearted, then one can find the Buddha in one's own asking. Furthermore, the appearance of the Buddha is not merely limited to human actions but also is unlimitedly found in all beings such as flowers, leaves, dark places, bright places, or even tiny dust-particles. What matters about any thing is its totality. A thing contains everything within itself. Nothing can be escaped from it without hurting to itself and to the escapee.

Case LXXXVI. Do Not Cherish Knowledge!

The holy light, that cannot be darkened, shines from time immemorial. One, who wishes to enter into this gate, should not cherish knowledge and explanation!

Xishan's Commentary

"The holy light cannot be darkened" is connected to the phrase mentioned in Case I, "bright and holy." "Shines from time immemorial" is connected to "It has no beginning and no end." "One should not cherish knowledge and explanation" is connected to "you should not cling to names when seeking explanations." "This gate" is the one through which any one, the unenlightened or the enlightened alike, is going out and coming in. As master Heze Shenhui said, the one word "to know" is the gate of all mysteries.

Having begun with the phrase "It has neither name nor form," this book ends with the phrase "One should not cherish knowledge and explanation." And thus it cuts a volume of tangles with this one phrase. However, this text begins and ends with explanations. Many practices set forth in between. Since the words "knowledge" and "explanation" are great poison to Buddhism, they were given special attention. This is the reason why Heze Shenhui could not become the legitimate son of the sixth patriarch.

Xishan's Poem

If the deepest meanings were shown like this,
That blue-eyed Bodhidharma from the west would burst out laughing.
However, what will be? Oh, what a pity!
The lone moon shines, while rivers and mountains are deadly quiet,
And roaring laughter frightens heaven and earth.

Blowing Rock's Commentary

Zen suggests to humankind that every attempt to reduce living reality to something knowable or explainable is a kind of obscenity. It is a violation of the mystery of life itself. It is an attempt to invade the ultimate privacy of One Thing found in all things and to parade It in Its nudity. Many truth seekers, like Shenhui, have asserted that they know what the universe is and have tried to explain it to people. Zen claims that there is something improper about that kind of approach to living things. Mystery is the soul of things. Whenever anything is alive, its core is mystery. When things lose their mystery, they die. The enlightened person does not demand of things that they surrender their mystery. One does not wish to conquer them utterly and to illuminate their every recess. Bodhisattvas, for example, allow life to keep its mystery. One loves, participates, and lives its mystery. Zen personality is quite different from the kind of cosmic peeping Tom who attempts to peer into the inmost secrets of the universe.

Humans must always remind themselves that only abstractions are clear. Reality in the concrete is mysterious. It is because one fears the concrete encounter that one turns away from reality and converts it into an abstraction. This obscenity is felt very strongly in most people who are avidly curious about the after-life or about communicating with spirits, and it infects a good deal of contemporary parapsychology. A Zen person does not seek to *know* and *explain* reality, instead one wishes to encounter it; that is, one wishes one's own life to be fully real. The heresy of Gnosticism is one against which all Zen people must forever be on guard. The gnostics content themselves with knowledge about reality. They remain in possession of a spiritual answer; they do not seek a truth, which is available only when it lives in one's self. Parenthetically speaking, I have often thought that Jung was a Gnostic rather than an authentically religious person. He seems more to want to *know* reality, to explain it, to conquer it by thought than to surrender to it.

To have an authentic relationship with anything that is living means that one encounters it in its mystery, and does not attempt to pry open its being. One relates to it as something infinite, and therefore never fully *knowable or explainable*. The wish to *know* the ultimate secret of life is the wish to conquer fate, or to be in control of life, or to be absolutely secure; in short, to be God. Moreover, it is the wish to have all these things without paying the price, without involving and without giving oneself. The wish to understand life intellectually stems from the desire to possess life while keeping oneself intact. And one likes to preserve oneself, remaining captain of all one surveys. But no one can relate in a living way to anything living and keep oneself intact. One cannot remain external to the mystery of life and penetrate its secrets. This is the deepest and the highest teaching of Zen. *The Bible* says, *Whoever finds his life will lose it*. Life is like a chaste woman, who does not bare herself to strangers, but will not hold anything from one who commits oneself to her in holy matrimony. So the mystery of life is not a code to be broken by some kind of cosmic cryptology. It is something with which one has to unite in spiritual marriage. The meaning of life is something one participates in only as one gives onself to it. When one assumes the role of spectators of life, then one loses the inner sense of life and grasps only as an abstract meaning. The limitation of a *spiritual knowledge* is that it purports to offer the ultimate truth without exacting the ultimate price. It presents the nature of things and the plan of salvation, and it makes these available to people at no cost. But if what Zen has said is correct, what can be made available in this way must necessarily be an abstraction and not the reality of life. *That is the reason why one should not cherish knowledge of life, but cherish its mystery.*

One Thing is not any thing for anyone to know objectively: It is *No-thing*. The life of Zen is to know that there is *No-thing* to know and to lament that it is so difficult to communicate this "*No-thing* to know" to others. This is the deepest thing in the whole world.

Siming Weizheng's Postscript

This book was written by the old master of Caoxi sect, Tuiyin. Alas! Buddhism has been degenerating for about 200 years. Buddhists, both from the way of Meditation and from the way of Teaching, have created different opinions about Buddhism.

Those who emphasized the Teaching have tasted the refuse and counted the sands at the seashore. They did not know the way to directly point to the soul of humans and to naturally enter the mind of humankind, which is beyond and above the five schools of teaching. On the other hand, those who emphasized the Meditation were naively boasting of their spiritual advancement and disregarded awakening by way of cultivation. They did not know how to cultivate their behavior after sudden enlightenment. In this fashion, the Teaching of Buddha and the Meditation of Buddha have been overblown with confusion. Gold is hardly distinguishable from sand. It is said in *The Yuanjiaojing:*

> Hearing that anyone is originally Buddha, people say that there is neither ignorance nor enlightenment. It is a small-minded opinion to reject the law of causation. Hearing that anyone can be cut off from ignorance only after a long process of cultivation, people think that they might lose original nature, as if the true nature would have become distorted. This is also a small-minded opinion.

Alas! How dangerous it is! Why has the Way not been transmitted in a right way? The chain of transmission like a single hair has tried to lift up a thousand pounds of weight, but was about to fail. Fortunately, the master had lived in Xishan for about ten years and watched and cared for a cow. Leisurely he studied about fifty *Sutras* and sayings of masters. He jotted down the phrases that were valuable and needful. Sometimes, he taught his disciples these selected phrases, as though a shepherd feeds the sheep with great care. He sat on anyone who progressed too fast. He whipped anyone who stayed far behind. In this way, he took pains to let them enter the great gate of enlightenment. Nevertheless, all his immature disciples complained that the words were highly difficult for them to comprehend. He took pity on them and made careful commentaries and orderly editing of each phrase. He made connections between various joints of phrases in one living stream to let the blood flow again. And thus both the essence of the 80,000 *Pitakas* and the original meaning of the five sects have been well expressed here. Every word having been so apt to both the principle and the central meaning, the lopsided became round again; the hooked became straight again. Indeed, his written words are the mirrors of both Teaching and Meditation. It is a good medicine for enlightenment and Cultivation as well.

However, the master worried about his single word or even his partial phrase being published for the world. He never wished his writings to be judged as his *magnum opus*. His student, Baihuan Puyuan, nevertheless copied the writings of Xishan with care. Biquan-Chande Yitian edited them. The masters, Dachang and Qingxia-Daoren Farong, admired them, saying, "Wonderful Indeed!" They with other six or seven friends spent all their money to put the words on the wooden plates as a way of repaying his teaching and his grace of enlightenment.

The subtle law of the patriarchs and the profound principle of the Buddha like the sea are deep and wide. Where could people find the coral and the priceless gem? If one's effort of searching in the sea is not as diligent as that of searching on the earth, one may merely sigh while watching the sea from the shore! Xishan's effort of selecting and his grace for enlightenment are as high as the mountains and as deep as the sea. Even if one's own body could be ground up a thousand times, and even if one's life could be given up 10,000 times, how could anyone repay even one tiny speck of his grace! If anyone from 1,000 miles away hears, sees, and accepts the writing as a treasure without fear and doubt, this book will certainly become a chunk of cloud.

Spring, the year of Wanlijimao(1579 A. D.)
Written by Siming Weizheng

Blowing Rock's Commentary

Weizheng was his priestly name, while his pen name was Siming. He was born in 1544 A.D., the thirty-ninth year of Zhongzong, the king of Li dynasty. He died in 1610 at the age of sixty-six. He was one of Xishan's favorite disciples.